THE CURTI LECTURES

The University of Wisconsin–Madison

October 1985

To honor the distinguished historian Merle Curti,
lectures in social and intellectual history
were inaugurated in 1976 under the sponsorship of the
University of Wisconsin Foundation and the
Department of History of the University of Wisconsin–Madison.

Spheres of Liberty

An 1849 U.S. silver dollar displaying the seated Liberty engraved by Christian Gobrecht. This popular and widely used design appeared on American coinage for more than half a century: on dollars (1836–73), half-dollars (1839–91), quarters (1838–91), dimes (1837–91), and half-dimes (1837–73). (Courtesy, National Numismatic Collections, National Museum of American History, Smithsonian Institution, Washington, D.C.)

Spheres of Liberty

Changing Perceptions of Liberty in American Culture

MICHAEL KAMMEN

Cornell University Press

Ithaca and London

First published, Cornell Paperbacks, 1989 by Cornell University Press.

Library of Congress Cataloging-in-Publication Data

Kammen, Michael G.
  Spheres of liberty : changing perceptions of liberty in American culture / Michael Kammen. — Cornell paperbacks ed.
      p. cm.
  Reprint. Originally published: Madison, Wis. : University of Wisconsin Press, 1986.
  Includes bibliographical references and index.
  ISBN 0-8014-9682-9 (alk. paper)
  1. Liberty—History. 2. Political science—United States—History. I. Title.
[JC599.U5K29 1989]   323.44'09—dc20   89-42934

Printed in the United States of America

⊗The paper used in this publication meets the minimum requirements of the American National Standard for Permanence of Paper for Printed Library Materials Z39.48–1984.

for Daniel Merson Kammen

Contents

Illustrations

Illustrations

Acknowledgments

I feel deeply honored and grateful to the Department of History at the University of Wisconsin–Madison, for its gracious invitation to present the Curti Lectures for 1985–86.

Benjamin Franklin is supposed to have said to Thomas Paine: "Where liberty is, there is my home." Whereupon Paine is supposed to have replied: "Where liberty is not, there is *my* home." Perhaps because the spirit of liberty already *is* in Madison, I felt very much at home throughout my visit there. Many people extended cordial hospitality, but I particularly wish to thank those who took a special interest in these lectures and helped to make my stay so congenial: Ann and Paul Boyer, Frances and Willard Hurst, William J. Courtenay, Sterling Fishman, Stanley I. Kutler, Michael MacDonald, George Mosse, Florencia Mallon, Steve J. Stern, and above all, Merle Curti himself, ever genial, gentle, and sparkling in spirit.

I would also like to convey deep appreciation to Allen N. Fitchen, Director of the University of Wisconsin Press; Elizabeth Steinberg, Chief Editor at the Press; Anne Eberle, who made the index; and to Corrinne Sheppard Eastman, who typed and retyped and proofread the manuscript with such expertise, dispatch, and good cheer. Three Cornell students assisted me during the research phase, 1983–85: Laura Dick, Matthew Berger, and Josh Joseph. Their co-operation was indispensable. I can only hope that it was an informative and interesting experience for them.

Five colleagues and friends read the essays with critical acumen and made useful suggestions for their improvement: Paul Boyer, Dennis Hutchinson, Isaac Kramnick, Fred Somkin, and Cushing

Acknowledgments

Strout. A sixth, Forrest McDonald, reviewed the manuscript with his own remarkable blend of empathy, erudition, and energy, and saved me from several gaffes, stylistic as well as substantive.

For assistance in tracing elusive leads pertaining to liberty in American iconography, I am indebted to Katherine Whitney at the Inventory of American Paintings, National Museum of American Art, a unit of the Smithsonian Institution; to Elvira Clain-Stefanelli, Executive Director of the National Numismatic Collections, National Museum of American History, also a unit of the Smithsonian; and Laurie Weitzenkorn, Assistant Curator at the Index of American Design, located at the National Gallery of Art in Washington, D.C. Ellen Baker Wikstrom, Director of the Hinckley Foundation Museum in Ithaca, has been extremely enterprising and accommodating in arranging for photographs to be taken of liberty-related objects in the museum's collection. My sincere appreciation to them all.

The young man to whom this book is dedicated made no direct contribution. His spheres include not only liberty but some beyond my ken—physics, sinology, and others. The dedication is no more (and no less) than an affectionate expression of paternal love and pride.

Above Cayuga's Waters   M.K.

Introduction

*

"There is no word that admits of more various significations, and has made more varied impressions on the human mind, than that of liberty."

Montesquieu, *The Spirit of the Laws* (1748)

"The object of history is instruction. The history of our country is the history of liberty; its two former periods may teach men how to acquire liberty, the last should teach them how to preserve it."

Joel Barlow to Mercy Otis Warren, December 29, 1810

"The idea of liberty is one which each epoch reshapes to its own liking."

Marc Bloch, *The Historian's Craft* (1942)

The purpose of these three essays is to provide a framework for understanding the meaning of liberty in American culture. Several basic assumptions have shaped my schematization, and it may be helpful if I indicate them at the outset.

The first pertains to the need to differentiate some of the major continuities and discontinuities in American perceptions of liberty. Abraham Lincoln began his Gettysburg Address by specifying that in 1776 "our fathers brought forth on this continent, a new nation, conceived in Liberty, and dedicated to the proposition that all men are created equal." However presumptuous it may be to modify or tamper with Lincoln's eloquent formulation, the fact remains that by 1776 American conceptions of liberty had already been developing for five or six generations. Several of those conceptions turned out to be remarkably durable, whereas others that emerged in the nineteenth and twentieth centuries were barely visible in 1776. Consequently I have devoted the first of these essays to the colonial and revolutionary periods; the second to the nineteenth century (writ long—the 1790s to the 1920s); and the third to the twentieth century (also writ long—the 1880s to the present).

Because of the need for a linear and historical context, I find myself particularly sympathetic to a statement written by Felix Frankfurter in 1949: "Great concepts like . . . 'liberty' . . . were purposely left [by the founders] to gather meaning from experience. For they relate to the whole domain of social and economic fact, and the statesmen who founded this Nation knew too well that only a stagnant society remains unchanged."[1]

My second basic assumption is that comparisons are helpful in order to clarify the particular configuration of attributes found in the culture of a given nation. There is compelling insight in a

---

1. *National Mutual Insurance Co. v. Tidewater Transfer Co.*, 337 U.S. 582 (1949), the quotation at 646, a dissenting opinion.

statement made in 1846 by Jules Michelet, the great French historian: "Pick at random the most liberal German or Englishman, and then talk to him of liberty. He will answer, 'Liberty.' And then just try to see what he means by it. You will then see that this word has as many meanings as there are nations."[2] In support of Michelet's pronouncement we might recall Lord Acton's aphoristic questions, raised at Cambridge in 1895 as part of his Inaugural Lecture on the Study of History:

> But what do people mean who proclaim that liberty is the palm, and the prize, and the crown, seeing that it is an idea of which there are two hundred definitions, and that this wealth of interpretation has caused more bloodshed than anything, except theology? Is it Democracy as in France, or Federalism as in America, or the national independence which bounds the Italian view, or the reign of the fittest, which is the ideal of Germans?[3]

Even so, it is inevitable that American notions of liberty should owe a particular debt to British sources. Edmund Burke clarified why on March 22, 1775, in a speech before the House of Commons called "On Conciliation with the Colonies":

> England, Sir, is a nation, which still I hope respects, and formerly adored her freedom. The colonists emigrated from you when this part of your character was most predominant; and they took this bias and direction the moment they parted from your hands. They are therefore not only devoted to liberty, but to liberty according to English ideas, and on English principles. Abstract liberty, like other mere abstractions, is not to be found. Liberty inheres in some sensible object; and every nation has formed to itself some favourite point, which by way of eminence becomes the criterion of their happiness.[4]

Burke is correct on two counts. First, because we cannot proceed very far with an inquiry about the American concern for liberty

---

2. Michelet, *The People* (1846; reprint, Urbana, 1973), 21.

3. John Emerich Edward Dalberg-Acton, *Essays on Freedom and Power*, edited by Gertrude Himmelfarb (Boston, 1948), 14.

4. F. G. Selby, ed., *Burke's Speeches On American Taxation, On Conciliation with America, and Letter to the Sheriffs of Bristol* (London, 1897), 80. In 1790 James Wilson of Penn-

and authority, liberty and property, and ordered liberty without becoming aware that the first two linkages found their genesis in seventeenth- and eighteenth-century Britain; and that the third had strong parallels in nineteenth-century Britain.

Second, because I believe Burke to be absolutely right in asserting that "liberty inheres in some sensible object." One of the central contentions of these essays, therefore, as well as their mode of organization, is that the meaning of liberty in America has predominantly been explained in relation to some other quality: during the colonial period, liberty and authority—followed yet overlapped by liberty and property; throughout the nineteenth century, primarily liberty and order, although liberty and property was revived for half a century (1884–1934) in the guise of "liberty of contract"; and finally, in the twentieth century, liberty and justice. Toward the close of Part Three I will have something to say, also, about liberty and equality.

It should become apparent as we proceed, if it is not already, that all of these coupled concepts do not share exactly comparable relationships. Liberty and authority as well as liberty and order were perceived as counterpoised sets of qualities which required that tension be maintained in order to preserve a viable balance. Liberty and property, on the other hand, along with liberty and justice, have usually been understood as complementary values: deprive or deny one, and the other is instantly in jeopardy. Despite this variability in their connective relationships, however, all four sets achieved the kind of cultural prominence that comes to popular slogans with broad appeal. That is why they may look, at first glance, like peas from a single pod even though they functioned,

---

sylvania quoted Burke to support the contention that he (Wilson) belonged to a continuum of people seeking "to prove the pedigree of our liberties." Robert G. McCloskey, ed., *The Works of James Wilson* (Cambridge, MA, 1967), 2:589. For a useful illustration of Burke's point from the modern literature, see Roscoe Pound, *The Development of Constitutional Guarantees of Liberty* (New Haven, 1957), four lectures delivered at Wabash College on the topics "In Medieval England," "The Era of the Tudors and Stuarts," "In the American Colonies," and "From the Revolution to the Constitution."

historically, as two different sorts of relationships: antipodal and compatible.

It should also become apparent that the shifting perceptions of liberty have undergone a phasing that is anything but precise and tidy. Historical sequences rarely are. The tension between liberty and authority was well recognized by the 1640s. The bonding between liberty and property began to be discussed intensively a generation later. Then both sets functioned, *pari passu*, in a highly meaningful fashion throughout the eighteenth century. Thereafter they lingered on, got partially redefined, and remain to this day as residual aspects of political discourse. Meanwhile the concept of ordered liberty first emerged in the United States at the end of the eighteenth century, became dominant for more than one hundred years, and persisted until the 1930s, when liberty and justice came into its own. Anticipations of liberty and justice had been in evidence ever since "Publius" (and more particularly James Madison) wrote *The Federalist Papers*, however, and the concept started to achieve prominence and vitality during the first third of the twentieth century.

Consequently it is necessary to acknowledge that although these pairings are developmental and sequential, although there are special dates when changes can be charted (such as 1789 and 1937), there has also been a lot of chronological overlap and intermingling that resulted from various causes, such as casual usage, political posturing, and judicial vacillation. Thus in 1808 a Federal district judge in Boston named John Davis could invoke the phrase "liberty, justice, and order"; and in 1920 an editorial praised "that great instrument [the U.S. Constitution] which has made our land the home of justice, order, and liberty."[5] Although such configurations of clustered use are not rare, neither have they been com-

---

5. Davis is quoted in R. Kent Newmyer, *Supreme Court Justice Joseph Story: Statesman of the Old Republic* (Chapel Hill, 1985), 118; editorial, "The Observance of Constitution Day," *Constitutional Review* 4 (January 1920): 46. See also John Adams's Special Session Message, May 16, 1797, in James D. Richardson, ed., *A Compilation of the Messages and Papers of the Presidents, 1789–1897* (Washington, D.C., 1896–99), 1:233; Horace White,

mon. The predominant pattern, by far, has been to employ one of the paired concepts, depending upon the era, the situation, and the ideological persuasion of the particular speaker or writer.

The fact that these concepts have not always had the same meaning for all Americans results partly from social diversity and partly from definitional vagaries. Lord Acton may have stretched a point for purposes of effect when he alluded to two hundred definitions; but he did not need to stretch his point very far. We may cite three statements in order to illustrate the on-going belief that defining liberty is a limitless exercise:

- *Montesquieu in* The Spirit of the Laws *(1748):*
There is no word whatsoever that has admitted of more various significations, and has made more different impressions on human minds, than that of *Liberty.* Some have taken it for a facility of deposing a person on whom they had conferred a tyrannical authority; others for the power of chusing a person whom they are obliged to obey; others for the right of bearing arms, and of being thereby enabled to use violence; others in fine for the privilege of being governed by a native of their own country or by their own laws. (Book XI, ch. 2)
- *Abraham Lincoln speaking in Baltimore, Maryland (1864):*
The world has never had a good definition of the word liberty, and the American people, just now, are much in want of one. We all declare for liberty; but in using the same *word* we do not all mean the same *thing.* With some the word liberty may mean for each man to do as he pleases with himself, and the product of his labor; while with others the same word may mean for some men to do as they please with other men, and the product of other men's labor. Here are two, not only different, but incompatable things, called by the same name—liberty. And it follows that each of the things is, by the respective parties, called by two different and incompatable names—liberty and tyranny.[6]

Speeches and Writings (Syracuse, 1932), 235, 238 (a speech given in 1912); *New York Times,* August 19, 1923, sec. 2, p. 5; Herbert Hoover, *The Challenge to Liberty* (New York, 1934), 3, 31; R. W. B. Lewis, *Edith Wharton: A Biography* (New York, 1975), 160.

6. "Address at Sanitary Fair, Baltimore, Maryland," April 18, 1864, in Roy P. Basler, ed., *The Collected Works of Abraham Lincoln* (New Brunswick, NJ, 1953), 7:301–2. The paragraph that follows the one just quoted provides yet another neglected example of Lincoln's oratorical brilliance. "The shepherd drives the wolf from the sheep's throat, for

Introduction

• *Sir Isaiah Berlin in his inaugural lecture at Oxford (1958):*
The essence of the notion of liberty, both in the "positive" and the "negative" senses, is the holding off of something—of others, who trespass on my field or assert their authority over me, or of obsessions, fears, neuroses, irrational forces—intruders and despots of one kind or another.[7]

The substance of these three essays will not only suggest that the meaning of liberty has changed and broadened over time, but that variant definitions have been subscribed to concurrently. Usages decline, but rarely do they disappear entirely. Above all, there has been an expansion of what is embraced by the concept of liberty, for, as Justice Potter Stewart wrote in 1972, "in a Constitution for a free people, there can be no doubt that the meaning of 'liberty' must be broad indeed."[8] The disadvantage of such breadth is that when liberty means different things to different people, it is likely to create difficulties in public dialogue whereby groups may misunderstand one another. A compensating advantage, however, is that interpretations of liberty have become more comprehensive, ranging from constraints upon authority to improvements in the conditions of social justice, of privacy, and a growing concern for the protection of personal liberty, particularly as prescribed by the Fourteenth Amendment.

The historical fact that liberty has indeed meant different things

---

which the sheep thanks the shepherd as a *liberator*, while the wolf denounces him for the same act as the destroyer of liberty, especially as the sheep was a black one. Plainly the sheep and the wolf are not agreed upon a definition of the word liberty; and precisely the same difference prevails to-day among us human creatures, even in the North, and all professing to love liberty. Hence we behold the processes by which thousands are daily passing from under the yoke of bondage, hailed by some as the advance of liberty, and bewailed by others as the destruction of all liberty. Recently, as it seems, the people of Maryland have been doing something to define liberty; and thanks to them that, in what they have done, the wolf's dictionary, has been repudiated."

7. Berlin, *Two Concepts of Liberty* (Oxford, 1958), 43. See also John P. Diggins, *The Lost Soul of American Politics: Virtue, Self-Interest, and the Foundations of Liberalism* (New York, 1984), 96, for the Lockean sense of liberty, so influential in the colonies and the early republic.

8. Stewart's opinion for the Court in *Board of Regents of State Colleges et al. v. Roth*, 408 U.S. 564 (1972), the quotation at 572.

to different people cannot be stressed too strongly. It has even meant different things to the very same people at various stages of their careers, or in situations that called for divergent emphases. Consequently, for example, the reader should not be surprised to find Theodore Roosevelt stressing ordered liberty in the second essay and liberty and justice in the third. There have been several "languages of liberty" (to borrow a felicitous phrase from J. H. Hexter), dating all the way back to antiquity. These languages converge from time to time; and Americans, in particular (having internalized aspects of them all), often utilized the legacy of those languages casually, even sloppily, and sometimes expediently.

The constraints of time and space imposed by the format of the Curti lectures have unfortunately precluded systematic discussion in this slender book of American attitudes toward religious liberty. Although I regret this omission, I take comfort in the knowledge that the development of religious liberty has already elicited a rich and reliable literature. The work of Anson Phelps Stokes, Leo Pfeffer, Mark DeWolfe Howe, Jr., William G. McLoughlin, Cushing Strout, and Nathan O. Hatch comes to mind immediately, though the list is exemplary rather than exhaustive.[9] Similarly the concept of Christian liberty, which pervaded Puritan thought in England during the 1640s and 1650s, especially that of John Milton, and which appears in the earliest political writing of John Locke, must await elaboration and analysis on another occasion.[10]

Although liberty has often been discussed in nonconstitutional contexts — by clergymen, politicians, journalists, and political theorists, for example — the most frequent and influential analyses in

9. See Stokes, *Church and State in the United States*, 3 vols. (New York, 1950); Pfeffer, *Church, State, and Freedom* (Boston, 1953); Pfeffer, *God, Caesar, and the Constitution: The Court as Referee of Church-State Confrontation* (Boston, 1974); Howe, *The Garden and the Wilderness: Religion and Government in American Constitutional History* (Chicago, 1965); McLoughlin, *New England Dissent, 1630–1833: The Baptists and the Separation of Church and State*, 2 vols. (Cambridge, MA, 1971); Strout, *The New Heavens and New Earth: Political Religion in America* (New York, 1974); Hatch, *The Sacred Cause of Liberty: Republican Thought and the Millennium in Revolutionary New England* (New Haven, 1977).

10. A. S. P. Woodhouse, ed., *Puritanism and Liberty, being the Army Debates (1647–9)*

the colonial period came from ministers and lawyers, and in the
national period from statesmen, judges, constitutional lawyers, political scientists and historians, often in response to problems of
legal exegesis.

Nevertheless, the nature of their analytical procedures has not
been adequately understood. In 1933 a newspaper editorial simply
asserted that liberty is the most important word in the Constitution because it is the basis for all other aspects of the document.[11]
A few years earlier, however, in commenting upon public perceptions of the Supreme Court, Felix Frankfurter observed that "the
meaning of 'due process' and the content of terms like 'liberty' are
not revealed by the Constitution. It is the Justices who make the
meaning."[12]

Because there is considerable truth to Frankfurter's remark, I
shall rely extensively in Parts Two and Three upon the opinions
of jurists; but by no means exclusively. In 1906 Justice Oliver Wendell Holmes wrote these prudent words of caution to his English
friend and correspondent of long standing, Sir Frederick Pollock:
"One who administers constitutional law should multiply his scep-
ticisms to avoid reading into vague words like 'liberty' his private
convictions or prejudices of his class."[13] Happily for the cultural
historian, those who administer constitutional law have not con-

---

... (Chicago, 1951), 59–60, 65–67, 80, 221–32; John Locke, *Two Tracts on Government*,
edited by Philip Abrams (Cambridge, 1967), 44, 129–30, 133–37, 139, 142–43, 218, 232. Locke
wrote these tracts in 1660–61. See also George L. Mosse, *The Holy Pretence: A Study in
Christianity and Reason of State from William Perkins to John Winthrop* (Oxford, 1957);
Oscar and Mary Handlin, *The Dimensions of Liberty* (Cambridge, MA, 1961), 58, 71.

11. "The Great Word" [Liberty], *New York Times*, September 17, 1933, sec. 4, p. 4;
and note the statement made by John Lothrop Motley in 1868: "Time will show that
progress and liberty are identical." *Historic Progress and American Democracy: An Address
Delivered before the New-York Historical Society . . . December 16, 1868* (New York, 1869), 44.

12. Frankfurter, "The Supreme Court and the Public," *The Forum* 83 (June 1930):
332. See also Frankfurter, "The Present Approach to Constitutional Decisions on the Bill
of Rights," *Harvard Law Review* 28 (June 1915): 791.

13. Holmes to Pollock, June 23, 1906, in Mark DeWolfe Howe, ed., *Holmes-Pollock
Letters: The Correspondence of Mr. Justice Holmes and Sir Frederick Pollock, 1874–1932* (2nd
ed.: Cambridge, MA, 1961): 1:127.

sistently heeded Holmes's caution. Consequently the prejudices of class and region, race and political circumstance permeate the opinions of jurists and thereby enable us to read them as vital signs of changing American values.

There is yet another reason why we are obliged to look to these disputes and decisions for evidence. With very few exceptions, Americans have not been inclined to undertake theoretical explications concerning liberty. We have nothing comparable to John Stuart Mill's *On Liberty* (1859), or Harold J. Laski's *Liberty in the Modern State* (1930), or Isaiah Berlin's *Two Concepts of Liberty* (1958).[14] The meaning of liberty in the United States has emerged primarily from political and judicial responses to practical problems; and as Felix Frankfurter reminded us, from applications of the Bill of Rights. He put it this way in an opinion for the Court (1943): "The history of liberty has largely been the history of [the] observance of procedural safeguards."[15]

When theory has been needed, the writings of John Locke, "Cato," Edmund Burke, John Stuart Mill, and others have been drawn upon (though not always cited). For the most part, however, theoretical expositions of liberty have been uncommon in the United States. The meaning of liberty has been defined by experience. Thomas Hutchinson said so in 1776. Walter Lippmann said so in 1920: "A useful definition of liberty is obtainable only by seeking the principle of liberty in the main business of human life, that is to say, in the process by which men educate their response and learn to control their environment." Justice Hugo Black said so in the broadest possible terms in 1941: "It must be recognized that public interest is much more likely to be kindled by a

14. In his Preface to *The Constitution of Liberty* (Chicago, 1960), Friedrich August von Hayek carefully pointed out that although he had lived in the United States for nearly ten years, "I cannot claim to write as an American. My mind has been shaped by a youth spent in my native Austria and by two decades of middle life in Great Britain, of which country I have become and remain a citizen" (p. vi). See also Herbert Butterfield, *Liberty in the Modern World* (Toronto, 1952); and D. D. Raphael, *Justice and Liberty* (London, 1980).

15. *McNabb et al. v. United States*, 318 U.S. 332 (1943), the quotation at 347.

controversial event of the day than by a generalization, however penetrating, of the historian or scientist."[16]

On those occasions when Americans have been inclined to generalize, a phrase used by John C. Calhoun and by Woodrow Wilson —"the sphere of liberty"—served as a handy *double entendre*. Sometimes it referred to how much or how little liberty has been available, in the sense of enlarging or diminishing "the sphere of liberty." At other times it referred to those related attributes that give more particular meaning to the spheres within which liberty is able to exist and serve the needs of humanity, such as physical security, or personal happiness, or economic opportunity, or government by law, or a just society.[17]

These have all been viewed as spheres of liberty at one time or another. They have sometimes circumscribed and sometimes enhanced liberty, which is why it is appropriate to say that spheres of liberty have expanded and contracted over the centuries. The American experience, overall, has been one of progress blemished by setbacks. If that is less than one might hope for, it is preferable to the obverse: a history of collapsing spheres marked by only occasional improvement. Viewed over a long period of time, and in comparative perspective, American spheres of liberty have expanded more often than not; and by doing so have brought the blessings of liberty—qualities of life and conditions that have been cherished universally, but nowhere more earnestly than in the United States. Chief Justice Earl Warren joined a distinguished line of predecessors when he described these aspirations in 1955:

> Faith in America confirms the hope that we shall preserve for our children all that our fathers, by the way of clear thinking, firm resolution, patient

16. [Thomas Hutchinson], *Experience Preferable to Theory. An Answer to Dr. Price's Observations on the Nature of Civil Liberty, and the Justice and Policy of the War with America* (London, 1776), esp. 15–19; Lippmann, *Liberty and the News* (New York, 1920), 68; Black's opinion for the Court in *Bridges v. California*, 314 U.S. 252 (1941), the quotation at 268.

17. John C. Calhoun, *A Disquisition on Government and Selections from the Discourse*, edited by C. Gordon Post (New York, 1953), 46; Woodrow Wilson, *An Old Master, and Other Political Essays* (New York, 1893), 83–84.

endurance and willing sacrifice secured for us; that our heritage of liberty will not dwindle but increase; and that we will prove worthy of what we have so abundantly received. It is such faith, I believe, that brings all of us together today to consider the 'Blessings of Liberty.'[18]

18. Warren, "Blessings of Liberty," *Washington University Law Quarterly*, vol. 1955 (April 1955): 111.

Part One

*

Liberty, Authority, and Property in Early America

". . . beset with those that contend, on one side for too great Liberty, and on the other side for too much Authority, 'tis hard to passe between the points of both unwounded."

> Thomas Hobbes, *Leviathan: Or the Matter, Forme & Power of a Commonwealth, Ecclesiasticall and Civill* (1651), from the dedication to Francis Godolphin.

". . . it frequently happens, that we cannot ascertain the degree of Liberty enjoyed by a community, by comparing the particular parts of a constitution, or the administration of it, with the abstract notion of Liberty."

> Nathaniel Niles, *Two Discourses on Liberty; Delivered at the North Church, in Newbury-Port, on Lords'-Day, June 5th, 1774* . . . (1774).

The concept of liberty did not appear often during the first few decades of English colonization in the New World. Between the onset of the revolutionary crisis in 1763 and ratification of the Constitution in 1788, however, no notion was invoked more frequently. Throughout the intervening generations, from the 1640s until the 1760s, liberty began to be discussed increasingly in the Anglo-American world, though not always precisely or systematically. It seems reasonable to assert that the colonists gradually "discovered" liberty during the seventeenth century, and then became obsessed by it during the course of the eighteenth.

Unluckily for those who like to have the history of ideas neatly packaged, liberty tended to mean different things in different situations. Moreover, the variations are not merely diachronic (changing usages over time), but also synchronic (divergent applications of the term occurring simultaneously). Provost William Smith of Philadelphia, for example, composed an important document in 1758 in which numerous references to liberty appear: several in connection with the concept of property—a common linkage—but others signifying personal freedom of movement, as opposed to incarceration—also a standard usage. In 1774 young James Madison congratulated a friend in Pennsylvania on his good fortune and happiness at

> dwelling in a Land where [the] public has long felt the good effects of their religious as well as Civil Liberty. Foreigners have been encouraged to settle amg. you. Industry and Virtue have been promoted by mutual emulation and mutual Inspection, Commerce and the Arts have flourished and I can not help attributing those continual exertions of Gen[i]us which appear among you to the inspiration of Liberty and that love of Fame and Knowledge which always accompany it.[1]

1. Peter C. Hoffer, "Law and Liberty: In the Matter of Provost William Smith of Philadelphia, 1758," *William and Mary Quarterly* 38 (October 1981): 681–701; Madison to William Bradford, April 1, 1774, in William T. Hutchinson and William M. E. Rachal, eds., *The Papers of James Madison* (Chicago, 1962), 1:112. A few months earlier Madison

Defining and clarifying the true nature of civil liberty emerged as one of the most compelling challenges for leaders of the revolutionary generation—more particularly the relationship of civil liberty to republican government and two esteemed qualities that it ought to protect and promote: property and happiness. On June 25, 1787, Charles Pinckney of South Carolina presented to the Constitutional Convention a speech on the character of the potential Union in which he explained that the purpose of republican government was the extension to its citizens of "all the blessings of civil & religious liberty,—capable of making them happy at home."[2]

Along with constant allusions to civil and religious liberty, we also encounter numerous references to liberty and authority, to liberty and property (which remained a popular slogan from 1689 through 1776), to "Liberty and Reason"[3] (predictable during the Enlightenment), along with several others, as we shall see. Liberty was clearly not a monolithic concept in colonial America. It could be used to convey diverse messages under varied circumstances. That should come as no surprise, however, because in early modern Britain liberty was scarcely a singular concept either; and the vocabulary of public affairs in early America was highly derivative from discourse at home.

Deviations did develop, especially in the years after 1776; but to appreciate those deviations, and to understand the complex evolution of liberty in American thought and culture, we must begin with its multiple applications in Stuart and Georgian England: the Tory concern for liberty constrained by law and authority; the

---

had asked Bradford to "pray for Liberty of Conscience" to be revived. See Hutchinson and Rachal, eds., *Papers of James Madison*, 106.

2. Max Farrand, ed., *The Records of the Federal Convention of 1787* (rev. ed.: New Haven, 1937), 4:28–29. See also John Jay to John Adams, July 4, 1787, in Henry P. Johnston, ed., *The Correspondence and Public Papers of John Jay* (New York, 1891), 3:248–49; George Washington to Thomas Jefferson, January 1, 1788, in John C. Fitzpatrick, ed., *The Writings of George Washington . . .* (Washington, D.C., 1939), 29:351.

3. See Rev. East Apthorp, *The Felicity of the Times. A Sermon Preached at Christ-Church, Cambridge, on Thursday, XI August, 1763 . . .* (Boston, 1763), 9. For "rational liberty" see Sean Wilentz, *Chants Democratic: New York City & the Rise of the American Working Class, 1788–1850* (New York, 1984), 84.

Whig protectiveness of liberty and property; and the radical or "Real Whig" notion, ultimately triumphant more than two centuries after its formulation by "Cato" in 1720–21, that the fulfillment of liberty should be found in social justice and in the broadest possible participation by citizens in public affairs.

Each of these linkages casts a very long shadow. Each one, modified or redefined, would still be in evidence during the later twentieth century. Their reciprocal relationships changed, however, and in that transformation we can watch the shifting values and priorities of a people. Could America become the "New Canaan of *Liberty*," an aspiration expressed in 1761 by one New England minister?[4] Yes it could, even though not all aspirants were permitted to enter, and some would do so only through their posterity. The process of change was slow, often painful and costly in human terms, but sometimes inspirational as well.

The process was also fraught with historical significance. Many Americans, much of the time, could not fully make sense of it. A few Americans, such as jurists, perhaps sought to make too much sense of it: they attached a particular meaning to liberty and said that that was it. *Voilà!* Meanwhile outsiders waited, watched with curiosity, sometimes tried to monitor the process and occasionally published their perceptions. Liberty viewed by Americans (as in a convex mirror) was subject to distortion. Liberty in America, viewed by foreigners (as through a telescope), may have been seen in clearer perspective but with essential details blurred or invisible. Hence the need to combine both visions, and to compare them.

Between about 1600 and 1750, discussions of liberty in Great Britain and her colonies were spasmodic, unsystematic, sometimes reductive and even inconsistent.[5] In the predominant line of thought,

4. Quoted in Sacvan Bercovitch, *The American Jeremiad* (Madison, 1978), 117.
5. See J. A. W. Gunn, *Beyond Liberty and Property: The Process of Self-Recognition in Eighteenth-Century Political Thought* (Kingston and Montreal, 1983), 230–31; James A. Henretta, *The Evolution of American Society, 1700–1815: An Interdisciplinary Analysis* (Lex-

natural liberty was undesirable and dangerous to security as well as to property. Consequently it seemed decidedly inferior to civil liberty. Therefore mankind willingly abandoned the unregulated freedom of natural liberty upon entering society and creating government. Variations on this theme abounded. One of the most familiar and fully developed occurs in John Winthrop's speech "On Liberty," given to the General Court of the Massachusetts Bay Colony on July 3, 1645. "The great questions that have troubled the country," he began, "are about the authority of the magistrates and the liberty of the people." Following an extended discussion of the former, he lectured the Court on the true meaning of liberty:

> For the other point concerning liberty, I observe a great mistake in the country about that. There is a twofold liberty, natural (I mean as our nature is now corrupt) and civil or federal. The first is common to man with beasts and other creatures. By this, man, as he stands in relation to man simply, hath liberty to do what he lists; it is a liberty to evil as well as to good. This liberty is incompatible and inconsistent with authority, and cannot endure the least restraint of the most just authority. The exercise and maintaining of this liberty makes men grow more evil, and in time to be worse than brute beasts: . . . . This is that great enemy of truth and peace, that wild beast which all the ordinances of God are bent against, to restrain and subdue it. The other kind of liberty I call civil or federal, it may also be termed moral, in reference to the covenant between God and man, in the moral law, and the politic covenants and constitutions, amongst men themselves. This liberty is the proper end and object of authority, and cannot subsist without it; and it is a liberty to that only which is good, just, and honest. This liberty you are to stand for, with the hazard (not only of your goods, but) of your lives, if need be. Whatsoever crosseth this, is not authority, but a distemper thereof. This liberty is maintained and exercised in a way of subjection to authority; it is of the same kind of liberty wherewith Christ hath made us free.[6]

Among the colonists Thomas Hooker of Connecticut also subscribed to that view, and in 1717 John Wise of Ipswich observed

---

ington, MA, 1973), 100; and see the eight major definitions, with historical illustrations, in *The Oxford English Dictionary* (1933), 6:240–42.

6. Perry Miller and Thomas H. Johnson, eds., *The Puritans* (New York, 1938), 206–7.

that "liberty does not consist in a loose and ungovernable freedom." It should be cherished yet kept under "due restrictions."[7]

In Britain we find variations on this theme in John Locke's *Second Treatise of Government*, in David Hume's essay "Of the Origin of Government," and in William Blackstone's *Commentaries*, three classics written between the 1680s and the 1760s. The most compelling strand of consistency in these texts, to my way of thinking, can be found in their sense of counterpoise. As Hume put it: "In all governments, there is a perpetual intestine struggle, open or secret, between AUTHORITY and LIBERTY; and neither of them can ever absolutely prevail in the contest. A great sacrifice of liberty must necessarily be made in every government; yet even the authority, which confines liberty, can never, and perhaps ought never, in any constitution, to become quite entire and uncontroulable."[8]

Throughout the eighteenth century, despite the development of variant and deviant formulations that we will examine in a moment, this orthodox view of the relationship between natural and civil liberty displayed remarkable tenacity. The assertion that natural law imposes duties and responsibilities respecting the liberties

7. For Hooker see Joyce Appleby, "The Radical *Double-Entendre* in the Right to Self-Government," in Margaret and James Jacob, eds., *The Origins of Anglo-American Radicalism* (London, 1984), 276; and for Wise see James Morton Smith and Paul L. Murphy, eds., *Liberty and Justice: A Historical Record of American Constitutional Development* (New York, 1958), 16–17.

8. See John Locke, *Two Treatises of Government*, edited by Peter Laslett (Cambridge, 1967), 301; David Hume, *Essays Moral, Political, and Literary*, edited by T. H. Green and T. H. Grose (London, 1889), 1:116; for Blackstone see Edward S. Corwin, *The "Higher Law" Background of American Constitutional Law* (Ithaca, 1955), 85. For a fascinating anticipation of Hume, see John Pym's 1641 comments upon the trial of Strafford: "The Law is the Boundary, the Measure betwixt the King's Prerogative, and the Peoples Liberty; whilst these move in their own Orbs, they are a support and a security to one another; the Prerogative a Cover and Defence to the Liberty of the People; and the People, by their Liberty, are enabled to be a Foundation to the Prerogative: but if these Bounds be so removed, that they enter into Contestation and Conflict, one of these Mischiefs must ensue: If the Prerogative of the King overwhelm the Liberty of the People, it will be turned into Tyranny; if Liberty undermine the Prerogative, it will grow in Anarchy." Quoted in Anne Pallister, *Magna Carta: The Heritage of Liberty* (Oxford, 1971), 7.

of others, and that without positive law there cannot be genuine liberty, permeated mainstream Whig thought, the Country Party ideology that legitimized opposition, and the broadly acceptable views of such conservative popularizers as Dr. John Shebbeare.[9]

In the American colonies, and even in the embryonic states during the decades following Independence, we continue to encounter this view in the writings of such divergent figures as Alexander Hamilton, James Wilson of Pennsylvania, and various clergymen.[10] In 1792, for instance, Timothy Stone, a Congregationalist minister from Lebanon, Connecticut, presented the election sermon before the governor and state legislature. "Some kind of government," he explained, is

> indispensably necessary for the happiness of mankind, that they may partake of the security, and other important blessings resulting from society; which cannot be enjoyed in a state of nature. . . . Civil liberty consists in the being and administration of such a system of laws, as doth bind all classes of men, rulers and subjects, to unite their exertions for the promotion of virtue and public happiness. A state of society necessarily implies reciprocal dependence in all its members; and rational government, is designed to realize and strengthen this dependance. . . .[11]

To summarize this enduring set of assumptions, then, no one had much to say of an approving character about natural liberty. It was invariably and pejoratively associated with the lifestyle of "savages" in general and American Indians in particular;[12] and every-

9. See H. T. Dickinson, *Liberty and Property: Political Ideology in Eighteenth-Century Britain* (New York, 1977), 65; Appleby, "The Radical *Double-Entendre* in the Right to Self-Government," 279; Gunn, *Beyond Liberty and Property*, 247–48.

10. See Forrest McDonald, *Novus Ordo Seclorum: The Intellectual Origins of the American Constitution* (Lawrence, KN, 1985), 2; Robert G. McCloskey, ed., *The Works of James Wilson* (Cambridge, MA, 1967), 2:587, 723–24, 767; Rev. Phillips Payson, election sermon to the Massachusetts legislature, May 1778, in John W. Thornton, ed., *Pulpit of the American Revolution* (Boston, 1860), 329–30.

11. Stone's election sermon is in Charles S. Hyneman and Donald S. Lutz, eds., *American Political Writing during the Founding Era, 1760–1805* (Indianapolis, 1983), 2:842.

12. See Montesquieu, *The Spirit of [the] Laws*, edited by David W. Carrithers (Berkeley, 1977), 201.

one agreed that civil liberty was a vastly preferable condition despite some sacrifices in the totality of freedom. Even James Wilson, who spoke more positively than his contemporaries about the "state of natural liberty," conceded in his *Lectures on Law* (1790) that civil liberty in a benevolent regime, such as republican government, offered categorical advantages. "True it is, that, by the municipal law, some things may be prohibited, which are not prohibited by the law of nature: but equally true it is, that, under a government which is wise and good, every citizen will gain more liberty than he can lose by these prohibitions."[13]

We should not be surprised that liberty and authority seemed such an attractively balanced ideal in colonial America, for current research suggests that the most common civil offense in the colonies was "contempt of authority."[14] Although these societies genuinely valued liberty, they nevertheless had considerable experience with excesses taken in its name, and with defiance of authority. The determination to resolve this problem throughout the nineteenth century would be rationalized in the name of liberty and order.

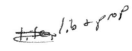

To those interested in revolutionary America in general and the Declaration of Independence in particular, no phrase is more familiar than "life, liberty, and property." For a very long time, the concept of liberty in English common law had meant freedom from personal restraint; or as Blackstone phrased it in his *Commentaries on the Law of England, Of the Rights of Persons*: liberty implied "the power of locomotion . . . without imprisonment or restraint, un-

13. See John Joachim Zubly, *The Law of Liberty. A Sermon on American Affairs, Preached at the Opening of the Provincial Congress of Georgia . . .* (Philadelphia, 1775), 6–7; Wilson, "Natural Rights," in McCloskey, ed., *Works of James Wilson*, 2:587.

14. I am indebted for this information to the work-in-progress of my colleague Mary Beth Norton, who has made an extensive analysis of the court records for colonial Maryland.

less by due course of law."[15] That limited usage for liberty, considered by itself, remained operative for purely legal purposes; but during the later seventeenth century the attractive linkage between liberty and property added a major dimension to public discourse.

The sacred trinity of life, liberty, and property is most closely associated with John Locke; it did not, however, begin with him. During the era of the English Civil War, Henry Ireton had insisted that property was the foundation for liberty; and in the subsequent generation, followers of James Harrington adapted Ireton's view and declared that property provided the principal security for liberty. By 1675 it had become almost a hackneyed phrase in Britain that property is "the highest right a man hath or can have to anything."[16]

Although John Locke devoted chapter five of his *Second Treatise of Government* to "Property," the most pertinent and influential passage appeared subsequently in the pivotal chapter entitled "Of the Ends of Political Society or Government." In response to the rhetorical question—If man is free in nature, why does he diminish his freedom and join society?—Locke explained that the enjoyment of man's property is insecure in a state of nature. Consequently man joins with others "for the mutual preservation of their lives, liberties, and estates, which I call by the general name, property."[17]

Unlike liberty and authority, then, which co-existed in a precarious equilibrium, liberty and property were highly compatible and required joint protection. Locke's comprehensive concept of property signified man's voluntarily circumscribed freedom in tandem with limitations upon the power of government. Taking Locke

15. See Henry Paul Monaghan, "Of 'Liberty' and 'Property'," *Cornell Law Review* 62 (March 1977): 411.

16. Lawrence Stone, "The Results of the English Revolutions of the Seventeenth Century," in J. G. A. Pocock, ed., *Three British Revolutions: 1641, 1688, 1776* (Princeton, 1980), 36–37; J. G. A. Pocock, "Machiavelli, Harrington, and English Political Ideologies in the Eighteenth Century," *William and Mary Quarterly* 22 (October 1965): 561–83; G. E. Aylmer, "The Meaning and Definition of 'Property' in Seventeenth-Century England," *Past & Present*, no. 86 (February 1980): 94–95.

17. *Second Treatise*, in Laslett, ed., *Two Treatises*, 368.

as a point of departure, however, various groups embellished the concept in ways that best suited their interests. When the mainstream Whigs spoke of defending the liberties of the people, they invariably meant protecting the privileges of men of substance. Even for lesser subjects, however, the most vital liberty concerned the right to protect their property from any arbitrary exercise of power or action against it. Man could be fully free only if he possessed property. The measure of an individual's right to participate in the political process, in fact, was his possession of real estate (and not just movable goods). Even the radical Whig spokesmen, Trenchard and Gordon, argued that liberty flourished best where the possession of property was widely distributed among a very substantial segment of the population. As "Cato" put it in 1721: "All Men are animated by the Passion of acquiring and defending Property, because Property is the best Support of that Independency, so passionately desired by all Men. . . . And as Happiness is the Effect of Independency, and Independency the Effect of Property; so certain Property is the Effect of Liberty alone, and can only be secured by the Laws of Liberty." The future reach of these intertwined themes remained quite extraordinary. During the later nineteenth century, Supreme Court justices in the United States would define liberty as the opportunity to acquire property.[18]

The earliest impact of this constellation of ideas in colonial America will be found in the writings and activities of William Penn. In 1670 he defined liberty and property by means of a simplistic explication of Magna Carta as a political symbol: "First, It asserts *Englishmen* to be free; that's Liberty. Secondly, that they have Free-holds, that's Property." In 1687 William Bradford of Philadelphia printed a pamphlet, *The Excellent Priviledge of Liberty and Property*, at Penn's behest. When the colonial rebellions occurred in 1689, liberty and property promptly emerged as a popular catch-

---

18. See Dickinson, *Liberty and Property*, 88–89, 160–168; David L. Jacobson, ed., *The English Libertarian Heritage: From the Writings of John Trenchard and Thomas Gordon in "The Independent Whig" and "Cato's Letters"* (Indianapolis, 1965), 177–78; Monaghan, "Of 'Liberty' and 'Property'," 435.

phrase to justify the usurpation of power that had been abused. In New England, for example, critics of Governor Edmund Andros charged that his actions between 1686 and 1689 had "invaded Liberty and Property."[19]

The phrase recurred throughout the next seven decades whenever a high-handed magistrate or authoritarian faction abused its prerogatives. In 1695 a New Yorker complained of Governor Fletcher's insulting disregard for the provincial Assembly, which the inhabitants regarded as the guardian of their "libertys and propertys."[20] In 1735 an essay written for *The New York Weekly Journal*, published by John Peter Zenger, declared: "As for property, it is so interwoven with liberty that whenever we perceive the latter weakened, the former cannot fail of being impaired."[21]

An essential point to keep in mind is that the political ideology being deployed during the first half of the eighteenth century was unabashedly British—a borrowing that Americans were glad to acknowledge. "Liberty & Property & No Wooden Shoes," a phrase commonly heard in the colonies, emerged as a popular slogan in England during the second half of the seventeenth century. It conveyed contemptuous allusions to absolute government, popery, and the conditions under which peasants lived on the continent.[22] In

19. Gunn, *Beyond Liberty and Property*, 230; Caroline Robbins, "The Efforts of William Penn to Lay a Foundation for Future Ages," in George W. Corner, ed., *Aspects of American Liberty: Philsosphical, Historical, and Political* (Philadelphia, 1977), 71; David S. Lovejoy, "Two American Revolutions, 1689 and 1776," in Pocock, ed., *Three British Revolutions*, 256; Increase Mather, *A Brief Account Concerning Several of the Agents* . . . (London, 1691), in Charles M. Andrews, ed., *Narratives of the Insurrections, 1675–1690* (New York, 1915), 276.

20. Roy V. Coleman, *Liberty and Property* (New York, 1951), 534. Coleman goes on to cite a charge made in 1707 by Samuel Jennings against Governor Cornbury of New York: "We cannot but be very uneasy when we find by these new methods of Government our Liberties and Properties so much shaken that no man can say he is the master of either." See also Christopher M. Jedrey, *The World of John Cleaveland: Family and Community in Eighteenth-Century New England* (New York, 1979), 131–32.

21. *New York Weekly Journal*, June 16, 1735 (no. 84).

22. I am indebted for this information to Professor Edmund S. Morgan of Yale University. See also Peter Karsten, *Patriot-Heroes in England and America: Political Symbol-*

1753, when George Mason, James Mercer, and James Scott drafted a "Proposal to Settle Foreign Protestants on Ohio Company Lands," they indicated that prospective colonists would enjoy religious liberty according to Britain's Act of Toleration, plus the naturalization privileges of English subjects, as well as the right to elect representatives, and concluded with a proud declaration that "the English Laws of Liberty and property are universally allowed to be the best in the World for securing the peoples lives and fortunes against Arbitrary power or any unjust Encroachments whatsoever."[23]

As the revolutionary crisis deepened, however, the phrase "liberty and property" was increasingly invoked, but with multiple meanings. In some instances the customary usage recurred: by both Sam Adams and John Adams, for example, that "Property must be secured, or liberty cannot exist."[24] In other situations the colonists insisted that they were defending English liberty (more particularly its well-established connection with property) against indifference and abuse by the King-in-Parliament. George Mason made this point while defending the Nonimportation Association in 1769. Starting in 1765–66 the Sons of Liberty took "Liberty and Property" as their slogan. Whenever someone recited it at a rally or meeting, the appropriate response was to huzza three cheers and hurl one's hat in the air.[25]

---

ism and Changing Values over Three Centuries (Madison, 1978), ch. 3, "'Liberty and Property': English Patriot Symbols in the Age of the American Revolution."

23. Robert A. Rutland, ed., *The Papers of George Mason, 1725–1792* (Chapel Hill, 1970), 1:28. See also W. B. Gwyn, *The Meaning of the Separation of Powers* (New Orleans, 1965), 16.

24. John Adams, *Discourses on Davila* (1790), in Charles Francis Adams, ed., *The Works of John Adams* (Boston, 1851), 6:279–81; Francis W. Coker, "American Traditions Concerning Property and Liberty," *American Political Science Review* 30 (February 1936): 5, 16; Adam Stephen to Richard Henry Lee, February 17, 1775, in Peter Force, comp., *American Archives*, 4th Series (Washington, D.C., 1837–46), 1:1244; Charles Royster, *A Revolutionary People at War: The Continental Army and American Character, 1775–1783* (Chapel Hill, 1979), 298.

25. "A Virginia Planter" [Mason] to the Committee of Merchants in London, June 6, 1766, and "The Nonimportation Association as Corrected by Mason" (April 23, 1769), in Rutland, ed., *Papers of George Mason*, 1:71, 103; [St. George Tucker], *Liberty, A Poem on the Independence of America* (Richmond, 1788), written in 1780–81; Coleman, *Liberty*

To complicate matters even more, however, between the later 1760s and the early 1780s other issues began to arise that would weaken the long-standing bond between liberty and property. Sometimes the precipitant might be a recognition (usually sparked when a slave brought suit for his freedom) that circumstances existed where liberty and property were incompatible. On occasion the precipitant was a feminist lament that woman's liberty was diminished when her property was arbitrarily controlled by her husband.[26]

Above all, debates over the new state constitutions, starting in 1776, exposed strains and unanticipated tensions between the newly expanded goal of political liberty and the traditional ideal that private property ought to be fully protected. Gouverneur Morris expanded upon this theme in a speech before the provincial congress of New York during the winter of 1776–77: "Where political Liberty is in Excess[,] Property must be insecure. . . . If the public be in Debt to an Individual[,] political Liberty enables a Majority to cancel the Obligation, but the Spirit of Commerce exacts punctual Payment." A divergence between property rights and political liberty also emerged from controversies over equal representation, that is, in the battle by newly settled areas with a less affluent population to gain seats in the state legislatures. Newer and poorer regions rejected the customary argument that the distribution of seats should be based upon the amount of property taxes collected in a town or county. "Taxation only respects property," would be the new egalitarian creed, "without regard to the liberties of a person; and if representation should be wholly limited by that, the man who owns six times as much as another would consequently have

---

and Property, 530–31; Michael Kammen, *Colonial New York—A History* (New York, 1975), 343–51.

26. See Levi Hart, *Liberty Described and Recommended . . .* (Hartford, 1775), 16, 20; William M. Wiecek, *The Sources of Antislavery Constitutionalism in America, 1760–1848* (Ithaca, 1977), 43; Abigail Adams to John Adams, June 17, 1782, in L. H. Butterfield, ed., *Adams Family Correspondence* (Cambridge, MA, 1973), 4:328.

six times the power, though their natural right to freedom is the same."[27]

The confiscation of loyalist estates during and after the Revolution, along with controversies (not to mention lawsuits) that they generated, deepened the fissure that had become apparent in the Lockean notion of liberty and property.[28] That familiar phrase would become comparatively quiescent in America for just about a century. Although it remained significant in constitutional law, it virtually disappeared as a popular political slogan. Liberty's linkage to other civic qualities became more urgent after 1789.[29]

During the Augustan Age—the second, third, and fourth decades of the eighteenth century—the concept of liberty was caught between cultural cross-currents that indicate both transition as well as ambivalence. On the one hand there is James Thomson's interminable yet symptomatic poem "Liberty" (1735–36), celebrating the revival of the goddess Liberty under benign Hanoverian auspices.

27. Willi Paul Adams, *The First American Constitutions: Republican Ideology and the Making of the State Constitutions in the Revolutionary Era* (Chapel Hill, 1980), 160–63; Adams, ed., "'The Spirit of Commerce Requires that Property Be Sacred': Gouverneur Morris and the American Revolution," in *Amerikastudien/American Studies* 21 (1976): 309–34.

28. See Harry B. Yoshpe, *The Disposition of Loyalist Estates in Southern New York* (New York, 1939); Catherine S. Crary, "Forfeited Loyalist Lands in the Western District of New York—Albany and Tryon Counties," *New York History* 35 (July 1954): 239–58; Beatrice G. Reubens, "Pre-Emptive Rights in the Disposition of a Confiscated Estate: Philipsburgh Manor, New York," *William and Mary Quarterly* 22 (July 1965): 435–56; A. Day Bradley, "New York Friends and the Confiscated Loyalist Estates," *Quaker History* 61 (Spring 1972): 36–39.

29. For comparisons with Great Britain, South Africa, and France in the later eighteenth century, see Dickinson, *Liberty and Property*, 318; George M. Fredrickson, *White Supremacy: A Comparative Study in American and South African History* (New York, 1981), 146; Donald R. Kelley and Bonnie G. Smith, "What Was Property? Legal Dimensions of the Social Question in France (1789–1848)," *Proceedings of the American Philosophical Society* 128 (September 1984), 200–230.

On the other hand a pervasive anxiety existed that excessive corruption could undermine liberty by debauching both the rulers and the ruled.[30]

Henry Care's *English Liberties* (first published in 1680), a collection of state documents such as Magna Carta and the Habeas Corpus Act, was reprinted from time to time and elicited mild interest, particularly in the colonies, where Americans often referred to their liberties (in sermons, pamphlets, and newspaper essays) but rarely defined them very precisely. Hence Francis Hopkinson's lament in 1754 that "an ignorant people would turn liberty to their own ruin, inasmuch as they would be in most cases free to act, and yet utterly uninstructed how to act."[31]

Amidst all of this uncertainty and ambivalence one striking development did emerge: a radical Whig interpretation of liberty that would eventually alter Anglo-American perceptions. During 1720–21 two British political writers named John Trenchard and Thomas Gordon produced a series of newspaper essays known as "The Independent Whig" and then a much longer run called "Cato's Letters." Thanks to Bernard Bailyn and others we now appreciate just how influential those essays were during the years of revolutionary crisis from 1765 to 1776. Their unmistakable impact appears in 1787 as well, for "Cato" seems to have been fond of the phrase "the blessings of liberty," which also appears in the Preamble to the U.S. Constitution.[32]

Although Trenchard and Gordon ranged across many different topics, the whole corpus of their work developed from a reconsideration of the meaning of human liberty. The pivotal essay, number 62 of "Cato's Letters," appeared on January 20, 1721, under

---

30. Alan D. McKillop, "The Background of Thomson's *Liberty*," *The Rice Institute Pamphlet* 38, no. 2 (July 1951).

31. Lawrence H. Leder, *Liberty and Authority: Early American Political Ideology, 1689–1763* (Chicago, 1968), 127–28; Hopkinson in *The Pennsylvania Gazette*, November 21, 1754 (no. 1352). Care's *English Liberties* had its fourth English edition in 1719 and its first American printing in 1721; the sixth edition was published in Providence in 1774.

32. See Jacobson, ed., *English Libertarian Heritage*, 176, 199.

the title "An Enquiry into the Nature and Extent of Liberty; with Its Loveliness and Advantages, and the vile Effects of Slavery." Cato began with a definition and then returned to it midway through the piece. As we shall see, his polemic is very much at variance with the liberty and authority "school," and deviates from the Lockean exegesis on liberty and property as well. Cato's emphasis upon individualism, happiness, and justice infuses these writings with notions and demands that would influence British radicals toward the end of the eighteenth century,[33] and would have immense implications—applied as well as intellectual—for Americans of the revolutionary era, the young republic, and beyond. "By Liberty," Cato began,

> I understand the Power which every Man has over his own Actions, and his Right to enjoy the Fruit of his Labour, Art, and Industry, as far as by it he hurts not the Society, or any Members of it, by taking from any Member, or by hindering him from enjoying what he himself enjoys. . . . True and impartial Liberty is therefore the Right of every Man to pursue the natural, reasonable, and religious Dictates of his own Mind; to think what he will, and act as he thinks, provided he acts not to the Prejudice of another.[34]

He then reached the point which sets his definition of civil liberty apart from those of his predecessors:

> Civil Government is only a partial Restraint put by the Laws of Agreement and Society upon natural and absolute Liberty. . . . Where Liberty is lost, Life grows precarious, always miserable, often intolerable. Liberty is, to live upon one's own Terms. . . . Liberty is the divine Source of all human Happiness. To possess, in Security, the Effects of our Industry, is the most powerful and reasonable Incitement to be industrious. . . . all Civil Happiness and Prosperity is inseparable from Liberty.[35]

In number 63, entitled "Civil Liberty produces all Civil Blessings, and how," Cato included a sentence that simultaneously identified

33. See Albert Goodwin, *The Friends of Liberty: The English Democratic Movement in the Age of the French Revolution* (Cambridge, MA, 1979).

34. Jacobson, ed., *English Libertarian Heritage*, 127–28, 130.

35. Ibid., 130, 131, 133, 135.

him as a "Real Whig" and anticipated the more egalitarian values of republican America in the years following Independence: "By the Establishment of Liberty, a due Distribution of Property and an equal Distribution of Justice is established and secured."[36]

The colonists would read and re-read these "libertarians" over an extended period of time. Some of their lessons took longer to be absorbed than others; but one lesson became immediately attractive and plausible because it described a political reality so familiar to Americans: the precarious relationship between power and liberty. An editorial prompted by the dissolution of New York's Assembly in 1747 summed up the situation in a sentence: "In all disputes between power and liberty, power must always be proved, but liberty proves itself; the one being founded on positive law, the other upon the law of nature."[37]

The antinomy between liberty and power would worry Americans intensely during the four succeeding decades. Sometimes they expressed their concern through the general context of national affairs and international relations, as in Abigail Adams's letter to Thomas Jefferson in 1787, while she lived in London and he served as minister to France: "To what do all the political motions tend which are agitating France Holland and Germany? Will Liberty finally gain the assendency, or arbitrary power strike her dead."[38]

More often, and more germane to this inquiry, they expressed concern in the particular context of devising adequate political institutions for the United States of America. Hence James Madison's hope that power could be conjoined with liberty under republican government. Hence Alexander Hamilton's comment to New York's ratifying convention in 1788 that the ultimate task in establishing a new form of government lay in the effort to achieve "the perfect balance between liberty and power."[39]

36. Ibid., 138.
37. *New York Evening Post*, May 25, 1747 (no. 131). For context and an extended analysis, see Bernard Bailyn, *The Origins of American Politics* (New York, 1968), 56.
38. Adams to Jefferson, September 10, 1787, in Lester J. Cappon, ed., *The Adams-Jefferson Letters* (Chapel Hill, 1959), 1:198.
39. See Adrienne Koch, *Power, Morals, and the Founding Fathers: Essays in the Inter-*

In 1789 David Ramsay of Charleston, South Carolina, wrote the first narrative and interpretive history of the American Revolution. In chapter two he explained why the patriots had been so attracted to the concept of liberty: "The reading of those colonists who were inclined to books, generally favoured the cause of liberty. . . . Their books were generally small in size, and few in number: A great part of them consisted of those fashionable authors, who have defended the cause of liberty. Cato's letters, the Independent Whig, and such productions, were common in one extreme of the colonies, while in the other, histories of the Puritans, kept alive the rememberance of the sufferings of their forefathers, and inspired a warm attachment, both to the civil and the religious rights of human nature."[40]

 civil pol libers

During the 1760s and 70s, the current condition and future of liberty became a compelling question in Great Britain—indeed, by 1776 it had developed as a major topic of debate. No consensus emerged, needless to say, because the range of opinion was so diverse. But discourse was stimulated by the Anglo-American dispute in general, and more particularly by a new argument that a few radical writers in the colonies touched upon casually while Joseph Priestley and Richard Price made it explicitly and systematically in England. They distinguished between civil liberty and an extension of it that they designated political liberty. By the former they meant the legally protected rights of individuals, especially protection of person and property. By the latter they meant the right of each man to participate fully in political life, and to give his consent to those decisions that would affect him. Radicals insisted that the maintenance of cherished freedoms depended

---

pretation of the American Enlightenment (Ithaca, 1961), 115; Gerald Stourzh, *Alexander Hamilton and the Idea of Republican Government* (Stanford, 1970), 5.

40. Ramsay, *The History of the American Revolution* (Philadelphia, 1789), in Hyneman and Lutz, eds., *American Political Writing during the Founding Era*, 2:723.

upon broad popular involvement in public affairs. Without such widespread participation, no form of liberty would be safe. Despite disagreements and controversies on both sides of the Atlantic, this new differentiation of liberty into its civil and political aspects marked an important step forward in theoretical discussion and democratic aspiration.[41]

In the most thoughtful and thorough assessment yet written about the concept of liberty in Britain during the American Revolution, J. A. W. Gunn has asserted that the distinction between civil and political liberty had only slight impact in the colonies, and that the patriots took their stand largely under the traditional banner of civil liberty even though the new notion of political liberty would have served them better.[42] I believe that Gunn has underestimated the impact of Priestley, Price, James Burgh, and David Williams in the new states, as well as the extent to which American polemicists even anticipated their arguments prior to 1776 and elaborated upon them thereafter. In 1765, for example, Martin Howard of Rhode Island explained that "I will shun the walk of metaphysics in my inquiry, and be content to consider the colonies' rights upon the footing of their charters. . . ." He preferred experience to theory. "I fancy," Howard went on, "when we speak or think of the rights of freeborn Englishmen, we confound those rights which are personal with those which are political: there is a distinction between these which ought always to be kept in view."[43]

41. Gunn, *Beyond Liberty and Property*, 229, 237, 241, 250–51, 258–59; Raoul Berger, *Government by Judiciary: The Transformation of the Fourteenth Amendment* (Cambridge, MA, 1977), 270. For a transitional formulation of civil liberty, poised between the traditional one and the new, see Nathaniel Niles, *Two Discourses on Liberty* (Newburyport, MA, 1774), 8.

42. Gunn, *Beyond Liberty and Property*, ch. 6, "A Measure of Liberty," esp. 251, 256, 258. Cf. Isaac Kramnick, "Republican Revisionism Revisited," *American Historical Review* 87 (June 1982): esp. 637–46.

43. See Bernard Peach and D. O. Thomas, eds., *The Correspondence of Richard Price* (Durham, NC, 1983), I, esp. 143–44, 149–51, 164–66, 188–91, 253–55; Howard, *A Letter from a Gentleman at Halifax . . .* (Newport, 1765), in Bernard Bailyn, ed., *Pamphlets of*

American emphasis upon participation and consent took different forms in response to varied situations. Benjamin Church defined liberty for a Boston audience in 1773 as "the happiness of living under laws of our own making." During the winter of 1776–77, moderately conservative Gouverneur Morris more pointedly devoted a separate section of an address to political liberty and defined that quality as "the Right of assenting to or dissenting from every Public Act by which a Man is to be bound. Hence, the perfect Enjoyment of it presupposes a Society in which unanimous Consent is required to every public Act."[44]

When Richard Price published his *Observations on the Nature of Civil Liberty* (February 1776), a defense of the colonists' dissenting position, it became an instantaneous bestseller. Few political pamphlets written in the eighteenth century stimulated more commentary and response. Over 60,000 copies sold during the first few months following publication in London. Despite numerous reprintings in England, supply could not keep pace with demand; and American reprints appeared promptly at Philadelphia, Boston, New York, and Charleston in 1776. Basically, Price regarded the traditional view of liberty as being merely a negative quality: Blackstone's definition of movement without restraint, and legal protection for individual rights; or, as the *Oxford English Dictionary* would have it, exemption from captivity, bondage, or slavery, and freedom from arbitrary, despotic, or autocratic control. Price offered a more positive and comprehensive analysis in terms of broad participation and self-government for the political commu-

---

the *American Revolution, 1750–1776* (Cambridge, MA, 1965), 1:535, 538. See also James Otis, *The Rights of the British Colonies Asserted and Proved* (Boston, 1764), ibid., esp. 441–70, "Of the Political and Civil Rights of the *British* Colonists."

44. Church, *An Oration Delivered March Fifth, 1773* . . . (Boston, 1773), in Hezekiah Niles, ed., *Principles and Acts of the Revolution in America* (New York, 1876), 35–36; Adams, ed., "Gouverneur Morris and the American Revolution," 329. See also Leder, *Liberty and Authority*, 123, where he quotes "Freeholder" writing in the *Maryland Gazette* on March 16, 1748, that one of the distinctive features of British liberty is the right of the people or their representatives to determine how much government should spend and on what. That right "is the great hinge upon which liberty hangs."

nity. Although Price aroused antagonists and did not carry the day at home, he nonetheless influenced fellow radicals to develop his expanded sense of the polity as well as the possibilities of political activism. David Williams's *Letters on Political Liberty* (London, 1782), for example, elaborated a similar distinction between civil and political liberty.[45]

The impact of Price, Priestley, and Burgh in America was immediate and strong precisely because the colonists had been moving toward similar conclusions for more than a decade. Benjamin Hichborn explained, early in 1777, that civil liberty was not "'a government of laws,' made agreeable to charters, bills of rights or compacts, but a power existing in the people at large, at any time, for any cause, or for no cause, but their own sovereign pleasure, to alter or annihilate both the mode and essence of any former government, and adopt a new one in its stead." As the war ended and attention turned from the destructive but necessary act of severing bonds to the creative work of establishing a new sort of polity, liberty and property were redefined and incorporated into this new notion of civil liberty revised to suit the nature of an expanding population living on a large land mass. A sermon given by Ezra Stiles in 1783 conveyed the widely shared sense that something fresh had appeared in the political firmament: "A Democratical polity for millions, standing upon a broad base of the people at large, amply charged with property, has not hitherto been exhibited."[46]

Is it any wonder, then, that a Frenchman who visited the newly independent states in 1777 took "*Liberty*, the basic principle of these

45. David O. Thomas, *The Honest Mind: The Thought and Work of Richard Price* (Oxford, 1977), chs. 8 and 10; Carl B. Cone, "Richard Price and the Constitution of the United States," *American Historical Review* 53 (July 1948): 730. See also Joseph Priestley, *An Essay on the First Principles of Government; and on the Nature of Political, Civil, and Religious Liberty* (London, 1768); and [Priestley], *The Present State of Liberty in Great Britain and Her Colonies* (London, 1769). For a wonderfully convenient compendium, see Bernard Peach, ed., *Richard Price and the Ethical Foundations of the American Revolution: Selections from His Pamphlets, with Appendices* (Durham, NC, 1979).

46. Peach and Thomas, eds., *Correspondence of Richard Price*, 1:151, 164, 189, 255, 270.

English colonies," as the central theme of his appraisal? Referring again and again to "this land of liberty" and "their love of liberty," he concluded that "their restive temper makes liberty, both in time of war and in time of peace, their main interest."[47]

James Wilson of Pennsylvania was just one among many who bore witness to the anonymous Frenchman's judgment. Between 1774 and 1790 Wilson often referred to the intense love of liberty among Americans, an affinity that he linked to the American character, respect for law, and a desire for popular rule by means of republican government. In the very first of his lectures on law (1790), Wilson defined the essence of American character in terms of "the love of liberty and the love of law . . . because neither of them can exist, without the other. Without liberty, law loses its nature and its name, and becomes oppression. Without law, liberty also loses its nature and its name, and becomes licentiousness."[48]

Wilson concluded his influential lecture, "Of the Law of Nature," with an optimistic observation that "the principles and the practice of liberty are gaining ground."[49] To which we should reply, "yes . . . but." Although Richard Price's reinterpretation of civil liberty found a responsive audience in America, its adherents dwindled during the post-war years. By no means did they disappear. Their voices emerge loud and clear from the Antifederalist literature. But events such as Shays's Rebellion looked to large numbers

Hichborn, *Oration, March 5th, 1777*, in Niles, ed., *Principles and Acts of the Revolution*, 47; Stiles, *The United States Elevated to Glory and Honor*, in Thornton, ed., *Pulpit of the American Revolution*, 415.

47. Durand Echeverria, ed., "The American Character: A Frenchman Views the New Republic from Philadelphia, 1777," *William and Mary Quarterly* 16 (July 1959): 386, 396, 398, 399, 400, 412–13.

48. McCloskey, ed., *Works of James Wilson*, 1:38, 70, 72.

49. Ibid., 146. The late Martin Diamond contended in 1975 that the founders "regarded liberty as a modern idea, as the extraordinary achievement of 17th- and 18th-century political thought." Considering the "new science of politics" in its entirety, Diamond's observation may be somewhat overstated. It is a useful reminder, nevertheless, especially because other aspects of the "new science of politics" have received more attention than liberty has in recent decades. See Diamond, "The Declaration and the Constitution: Liberty, Democracy and the Founders," *The Public Interest* 41 (Fall 1975): 47.

of anxious Americans like a vicious abuse of republican liberty—
and therefore an omen. The achievement of republican liberty had
to be balanced by national "energy" and the maintenance of social
stability. By 1787, when the Constitutional Convention met, the
concept of political liberty, arising from broadly based and *on-going*
participation, seemed somewhat less attractive than it had in 1776.
References to liberty narrowed once again to the protection of individual rights against encroachment by government, especially the
legislature.⁵⁰

Liberty continued to be an American by-word amidst the end-
less explorations of political theory that occurred during 1787–88;
but for many people its boundaries had contracted. Indeed, the
connections between liberty and authority as well as liberty and
property underwent a revival of sorts. A significant reorientation
took place in American political thought during 1787–88.

Const. Conv.

In the process of writing the Constitution and debating it for
ratification, liberty required discussion in four separate contexts:
whether it would receive more adequate protection if a strict separation of powers could be achieved; whether its symbiotic relationship to property would be sufficiently promoted under the new
instrument of government; whether the "happiness" hoped for in
the new nation would be realized under its auspices; and finally,
whether, as the Antifederalists maintained, a "consolidation" of
power would diminish the condition of liberty in the states and
consequently for individual Americans. Although each of these de-
manded discrete consideration, they interacted and overlapped in
complicated ways.

Those who framed the Constitution drew most heavily for guid-

50. Gordon S. Wood, *The Creation of the American Republic, 1776–1787* (Chapel Hill,
1969), 24, 412, 608–9; Gunn, *Beyond Liberty and Property*, 256. For Madison's explicit ac-
knowledgment of the tension between republican liberty and the need for energy and
stability in government, see *The Federalist*, numbers 37 and 63.

ance upon the American experience with political realities during the preceding quarter of a century. In so far as they heeded intellectual influences, especially external ones, a single source is cited more than all others combined: Montesquieu's *Spirit of the Laws* (1748). It should be acknowledged directly that that influential work enhanced the meaning of liberty by clarifying the distinction between freedoms embodied in a constitution as a system of government (liberty inherent in the procedures of a state) and the freedoms to which private persons were entitled by natural right and custom.[51]

It must also be noticed, however, that Montesquieu's belief that the preservation of liberty required a strict separation of powers was based upon a curious misunderstanding of the British constitution he so admired. Montesquieu had been strongly influenced by Locke's *Second Treatise of Government*, which was published in French as early as 1691. As Montesquieu matured, however, his views about the ideal polity went well beyond Locke; and the most significant factor in this process of development was Montesquieu's visit to England early in the 1730s. It is a commonplace that he came away with complete admiration for the British system, and regarded that constitution as the *ne plus ultra* in the entire history of governmental achievement.[52]

What is not commonly acknowledged, however, is the anomalous relationship between the conclusions Montesquieu reached and the constitutional tendencies that actually emerged during Sir Robert Walpole's durable regime. Somehow, Montesquieu seems to have understood law and formal institutions far better than he did the informal mechanisms of politics; because the dominant trend throughout the Whig ascendancy was toward a converging and blending of political power. The ministerial system, the mechanism known as King-in-Parliament, and the notorious pattern of patron-

---

51. See Gunn, *Beyond Liberty and Property*, 237; Paul M. Spurlin, *Montesquieu in America, 1760–1801* (Baton Rouge, 1940), ch. 6.

52. Robert Shackleton, *Montesquieu: A Critical Biography* (Oxford, 1961), 284, 286–87; Gwyn, *The Meaning of the Separation of Powers*, 11.

age all worked in such a way that authority tended to be concentrated rather than well distributed. While Montesquieu was in England the separation of powers was a partisan plea rather than a political reality. He nevertheless assumed that Britain's constitution owed much of its greatness to the separation of power in practice. Consequently Montesquieu dignified and rationalized the concept, attached it to his own theory of political liberty "and handed it to posterity as a doctrine far more practical than its proponents had known."[53] Here is the way he explained it in Book XI, chapter 6, "Of the Constitution of England":

> The political liberty [despite the misleading translation, he actually meant civil liberty] of the subject is a tranquillity of mind, arising from the opinion each person has of his safety. In order to have this liberty, it is requisite the government be so constituted as one man need not be afraid of another. When the legislative and executive powers are united in the same person, or in the same body of magistracy, there can be then no liberty; because apprehensions may arise, lest the same monarch or senate should enact tyrannical laws, to execute them in a tyrannical manner. Again, there is no liberty, if the power of judging be not separated from the legislative and executive powers. Were it joined with the legislative, the life and liberty of the subject would be exposed to arbitrary control; for the judge would be then the legislator.[54]

All of which contributed to a strange yet significant development in the history of American political culture. In 1787 the founders were spellbound by a misguided French reading of the British constitution as an ideal system for the salvation of liberty in former colonies where the British constitution had not been quite apt and had not functioned very smoothly. In a letter filled with criticisms of the new American Constitution, Jefferson wrote Madison late in 1787 that "I like the organization of the government into Legislative, Judiciary and Executive . . . and I like the negative given to the Executive with a third of either house." Madison made the point even more explicit in the forty-seventh *Federalist*, dated

53. Shackleton, *Montesquieu*, 298–301.
54. Montesquieu, *Spirit of [the] Laws*, 202.

January 30, 1788: "The preservation of liberty requires, that the three great departments of power should be separate and distinct. The oracle who is always consulted and cited on this subject, is the celebrated Montesquieu. If he be not the author of this invaluable precept in the science of politics, he has the merit at least of displaying and recommending it most effectually to the attention of mankind." Madison returned to this theme once again in *Federalist* number 51.[55]

Another major theme of *The Federalist Papers*, announced in the first issue and elaborated in the last, was the widely shared view that adoption of this new governmental scheme would enhance the preservation of liberty and property—a concern that became relatively quiescent between 1776 and 1787, but certainly did not disappear from view.[56] As Hamilton explained in *Federalist* number 85:

> The additional securities to republican government, to liberty and to property, to be derived from the adoption of the plan under consideration, consist chiefly in the restraints which the preservation of the union will impose on local factions and insurrections, and on the ambition of powerful individuals in single states, who might acquire credit and influence enough, from leaders and favorites, to become the despots of the people.[57]

55. Jefferson to Madison, December 20, 1787, in Julian P. Boyd, ed., *The Papers of Thomas Jefferson* (Princeton, 1955), 12:439, 440; Jacob E. Cooke, ed., *The Federalist* (Middletown, CT, 1961), 324–25, 348.

56. See Adams, ed., "Gouverneur Morris and the American Revolution," 316, 329–31; Robert F. Berkhofer, Jr., *The White Man's Indian: Images of the American Indian from Columbus to the Present* (New York, 1978), 48, 148.

57. Cooke, ed., *The Federalist*, 588. John P. Diggins has recently suggested that "in the *Federalist* attitudes toward liberty and property as rights also undergo a subtle but significant change, indeed a transformation that marks the passing of classical politics and the advent of a Humean perspective that modifies both the Lockean and Whig paradigms." Diggins, *The Lost Soul of American Politics: Virtue, Self-Interest, and the Foundations of Liberalism* (New York, 1984), 60–61, 97, 102. I am rather skeptical, in part because "Publius" never once, in all eighty-five *Federalist Papers*, mentions Hume by name, and he quotes from Hume just once in order to support a point having nothing whatever to do with liberty and property. When "Publius" wanted to cite an authority (such as Montesquieu) for intellectual reinforcement, he did not hesitate to do so explicitly.

During the Convention Hamilton had argued that inequities in the distribution of property necessarily resulted from liberty, a sentiment shared by Rufus King, John Rutledge, and Gouverneur Morris. Speaking at the Convention on July 5, 1787, in fact, Morris had gone to the unusual extreme of separating liberty and property as interdependent values. "Men don't unite for liberty or Life," he insisted, "they possess both in the savage state[.] in the highest perfection they unite for the *protection of property*."[58] I do not know that Morris possessed a more deeply felt bourgeois ethos than his colleagues, even though he frequently expressed strong concern for the "spirit of commerce." Nevertheless, his position seems to have been extreme. Far more common was the belief that liberty and property were so closely allied that a clear distinction could not be made between the two. Most Americans, Federalists as well as Antifederalists, shared the view that an "affinity" existed between them.[59]

Despite the widely held assumption that liberty and property shared a special affinity, and despite the assumption that government had a particular responsibility to safeguard both liberty and property, it is not true that happiness — as in Jefferson's resounding phrase, "Life, Liberty and the pursuit of Happiness" — was a puffed-up euphemism for property. Some members of the revolutionary generation did indeed use it casually in that way, but abundant evidence indicates that there has been needless confusion about this point.[60] Three sorts of materials can be brought to bear in support of this contention.

The first sort shows that for a very long time after 1776, when

58. See Drew R. McCoy, *The Elusive Republic: Political Economy in Jeffersonian America* (Chapel Hill, 1980), 133; Farrand, ed., *Records of the Federal Convention*, 1:536.

59. Farrand, ed., *Records of the Federal Convention*, 1:147; Herbert J. Storing, *What the Anti-Federalists Were For* (Chicago, 1981), 15, 66; Hyneman and Lutz, eds., *American Political Writing during the Founding Era*, 2:926, 934; Frank Tariello, Jr., *The Reconstruction of American Political Ideology, 1865–1917* (Charlottesville, 1982), 13–14.

60. For a valiant attempt to trace what Americans have meant by this most elusive (as well as allusive) phrase, see Howard Mumford Jones, *The Pursuit of Happiness* (Ithaca, 1953). See Forrest McDonald, *Alexander Hamilton: A Biography* (New York, 1979), 53–

Americans *meant* property, they *said* property rather than happiness, even when a felicitous or altruistic phrase would have been congenial to their purposes. Let us look at the example of Jefferson himself, who did not hesitate to invoke happiness when that is what he really had in mind. In his first annual message to Congress, December 8, 1801, Jefferson expressed the belief that most American citizens expected government "to establish principles and practices of administration favorable to the security of liberty and property"; and four years later Jefferson pledged himself once again to safeguard those rights.[61] James Madison used similar language on several occasions. So did justices of the Supreme Court, as well as men like Chancellor Kent of New York (who chose his words with care) and Jedidiah Morse, a New England Calvinist minister and patriot who wrote this conventional yet characteristic declaration in 1824: "By our improvements, and experience, the great truth has been fully and incontrovertibly established, that mankind are capable of self government; that liberty is compatible with individual security of person and property."[62]

A second category of evidence involves the numerous instances when happiness and property are used in the same breath, so to speak, with property (more often than not) subsumed as one among several important qualities that sustained happiness — clearly regarded as the ultimate quality. Thus this statement (dated November 1, 1787) from the "Essays of Brutus," one of the most penetrating Antifederalist writers: "The powers, rights, and authority, granted to the general government by this constitution, are as com-

---

54, for an excellent discussion of Vattel on happiness. Vattel echoed Burlamaqui, who very likely affected Jefferson's use of "happiness."

61. James D. Richardson, ed., *A Compilation of the Messages and Papers of the Presidents, 1789–1897* (Washington, D.C., 1896–99), 1:332, 388; Garry Wills, *Inventing America: Jefferson's Declaration of Independence* (Garden City, NY, 1978), 149–64.

62. Richardson, ed., *Messages and Papers of the Presidents*, 1:481; Charles Warren, *The Supreme Court in United States History* (Boston, 1922), 1:276–77; Dixon Ryan Fox, *The Decline of Aristocracy in the Politics of New York, 1801–1840* (New York, 1919), 254; Morse, *Annals of the American Revolution; Or, A Record of Their Causes and Events* (Hartford, 1824), 399.

plete, with respect to every object to which they extend, as that of any state government—It reaches to every thing which concerns human happiness—Life, liberty, and property."[63]

The third sort of documentation can serve as a capstone to this exploration of the varied meanings and uses of liberty in early American history: the fact that happiness *in conjunction with liberty* was acknowledged as an essential social goal long before 1776. Back in 1721 "Cato's Letters" had insisted that "Liberty is the divine Source of all human Happiness," a theme that another of Cato's namesakes, the anonymous New York Antifederalist (possibly George Clinton) explored in 1787: "My object is to take up this new form of national government—compare it with the experience and the opinions of the most sensible and approved political authors—and to shew, that its principles, and the exercise of them, will be dangerous to your liberty and happiness."[64]

This became a persistent *leitmotif* in Antifederalist literature throughout 1787–88: "Essays of an Old Whig," printed in Philadelphia's *Independent Gazetteer*; "Essays by [a pseudonymous] William Penn," published by the same paper in January 1788; and "Essays by the Impartial Examiner," which appeared in the *Virginia Independent Chronicle* during the first half of 1788, where the author defines "the great ends of human happiness" as "the preservation of their *natural rights and liberties.* . . ."[65]

Although expressions of that sort seem to have peaked in frequency as well as intensity between 1776 and 1788, it should come

---

63. Herbert J. Storing, ed., *The Complete Anti-Federalist* (Chicago, 1981), 2:374. For other examples from this period of the clear distinction between property and happiness, see John P. Kaminski and Gaspare J. Saladino, eds., *Commentaries on the Constitution, Public and Private, November 8 to December 17, 1787,* vol. 14 of *The Documentary History of the Ratification of the Constitution* (Madison, 1983), 3, 20, 24, 74, 297; and Rutland, ed., *Papers of George Mason,* 2:768, 770, 774, and 776, where Mason's correspondence for 1783 is crammed with this sort of statement: "The Establishment of American Liberty & Independence has placed Happiness & Prosperity within our Reach . . ." (776).

64. Jacobson, ed., *English Libertarian Heritage,* 133–34; Storing, ed., *The Complete Anti-Federalist,* 2:109.

65. Storing, ed., *The Complete Anti-Federalist,* 3:21, 170; 5:174, 198. Italics in the original.

as no surprise that this linkage between liberty and happiness ante-dated 1776. John Locke, after all, had warned that care in not mis-taking "imaginary for real happiness is the necessary foundation of our liberty."[66] George Mason of Virginia, for example, in public as well as private correspondence throughout 1769–70, repeatedly referred to "the Liberty and Happiness of our Posterity," and "the Liberty & Happiness of a Country." In 1788 those phrases recur once again in Mason's explanation to Jefferson of his refusal to sign the Constitution and in Mason's appeal that Virginia's ratifying convention reject the Constitution: "Here behold the difference between a powerful great consolidation and a confederacy. They tell us, that if we be powerful and respectable abroad, we shall have liberty and happiness at home. Let us secure that liberty—that happiness first, and we shall then be respectable."[67]

"Consolidation," as scholars have long been aware, loomed as the quintessential fear of the Antifederalists—and a genuine source of anxiety; but it was a negative attribute in their view, the char-acteristic or consequence that they most dreaded in the proposed Constitution. The positive attribute that they cherished ardently, and the one that they refer to most frequently, is liberty. Often as not they barely attempted to define it, though few were so can-did as "William Penn" about the problematic aspects of explaining liberty. "Here a long agitated question will occur," he conceded: "*What is liberty?* What is that supreme good which every one feels, and so very few can define?—I would call it *the unlimited power of doing good,* and without very critically examining into this defi-nition, I know not what internal voice tells me that I am not mistaken."[68]

When these opposition writers and spokesmen in the state rati-fying conventions sought to be more specific, their views were most commonly Lockean and traditional. Liberty is the obverse of slav-

66. See Jones, *Pursuit of Happiness,* 94–96. The quotation is from Locke's *Essay Concerning Human Understanding.*
67. Rutland, ed., *Papers of George Mason,* 1:108, 118, 119; 3:1044, 1065.
68. Storing, ed., *The Complete Anti-Federalist,* 3:169–70. Italics in the original.

ery (Luther Martin of Maryland); liberty is the objective of government (Patrick Henry of Virginia); "Liberty, in its genuine sense, is security to enjoy the effects of our honest industry and labours, in a free and mild government, and personal security from all illegal restraints" (The Federal Farmer).[69]

Many Antifederalists trotted through the inevitable process whereby the unlimited freedom of natural liberty must give way to the circumscribed freedom of civil liberty. To create a government for the common good, concessions had to be made; but mankind need not surrender *all* of its natural liberty. Those polemicists with a more cynical regard for human nature, however, made the realistic concession that there exist "certain inherent rights pertaining to all mankind in a state of natural liberty, which through the weakness, imperfection, and depravity of human nature cannot be secured in that state."[70]

On occasion, however, the special sense of political liberty that had surfaced so vigorously in 1776 reappeared. Writing as "Agrippa" in the *Massachusetts Gazette* on Christmas Day 1787, James Winthrop asserted that civil liberty "consists" in the consciousness that persons and property are secure, "and is best guarded by political liberty, which is the share that every citizen has in the government." An author called "Republicus," writing in the (Lexington) *Kentucky Gazette*, went further than most in an egalitarian direction. After admitting that civil government was needed because of man's passions, he provided a sketch of liberty that included innovative alongside traditional attributes: the enjoyment and protection of property, the power of self-government, and "a perfect natural equality among mankind."[71]

James Lincoln of South Carolina could not have been more succinct in answering his own rhetorical questions. "What have you been contending for these ten years past? Liberty! What is Liberty? The power of governing yourselves. If you adopt this Constitu-

69. Ibid., 2:35, 212, 261. See also Henry, ibid., 5:223.
70. Ibid., 2:373; 3:33, 182; 5:175.
71. Ibid., 4:84; 5:161.

tion, have you this power? No." Those who did reflect historically on the changes wrought by a tumultuous decade (actually longer) emerged with divergent responses. According to John Dawson of Virginia, had the Constitution "been presented to our view ten years ago . . . it would have been considered as containing principles incompatible with republican liberty, and therefore doomed to infamy." By providing the national Congress with too much power, the new Constitution seemed likely to be oppressive.[72]

Just a few of the Antifederalists who addressed liberty as their central theme were both realistic and candid enough to admit why the Convention of 1787 had been called, and why its product enjoyed strong support. "At the time of forming the Confederation," wrote "Cornelius" in Hampshire, Massachusetts, "the publick rage was on the side of liberty. The reigning disposition then was, to secure the highest degrees of liberty to the people. . . . The consequence is, want of sufficient energy in government. We have had a surfeit of liberty; and to many, the very name has now become nauseous."[73]

Those who supported the new Constitution did so for diverse reasons and combinations of reasons, ranging from the need for greater strength in foreign relations to a yearning for growth and prosperity rather than economic stagnation. But anxiety over "a surfeit of liberty" was genuine and widely shared, though people responded to it in various ways. What had transpired between 1776 and 1787 made Mercy Otis Warren, for example, feel very pessimistic about the future of liberty:

> Few had yet formed any adequate ideas, and fewer indeed were sensible, that though the name of *liberty* delights the ear, and tickles the fond pride of man,

72. Jonathan Elliot, ed., *The Debates in the Several State Conventions on the Adoption of the Federal Constitution* . . . (2nd ed.: Philadelphia, 1876), 3:607; 4:313.

73. Storing, ed., *The Complete Anti-Federalist*, 4:144.

it is a jewel[74] much oftener the play-thing of his imagination, than a possession of real stability. . . . This is the usual course of human conduct, however
painful the reflection may be to the patriot in retirement, and to the philosopher absorbed in theoretic disquisitions on human liberty, or the portion
of natural and political freedom to which man has a claim. . . . Thus by habit
they are ready to believe, that mankind in general are incapable of the enjoyment of that liberty which nature seems to prescribe. . . .[75]

Warren concluded her history of the revolutionary epoch with
a bitter denunciation of the Constitution and a populist blast at
the founders because the Convention had met in secret. "Many
of the intelligent yeomanry and of the great bulk of independent
landholders," she added, "who had tasted the sweets of mediocrity,
equality, and liberty, read every unconditional ratification of the
new system in silent anguish. . . ." In the last analysis, Warren argued, ratification would not have occurred without the presump-
tion that a bill of rights would swiftly follow: "It is evident that
a majority of the states were convinced that the constitution, as
at first proposed, endangered their liberties."[76]

The Fifth Amendment in the Bill of Rights, passed by Congress
in September 1789 and ratified by the states in December 1791, did
prohibit the Federal government from depriving any person of
"life, liberty, or property, without due process of law"; and presumably the Antifederalists felt sanguine that state laws or bills of rights
would provide comparable protection for liberty at levels lower than
the national.[77] Even so, those who felt most apprehensive about
that "surfeit of liberty" and its implications found themselves attracted once again to the conceptual coupling of liberty and authority. Looking back from the 1830s, Tocqueville remarked that

74. The favorite metaphors and images used in association with liberty were goddess, jewel, and altar. See ibid., 2:171; Elisha Williams, *The essential Rights and Liberties
of Protestants. A seasonable Plea for the Liberty of Conscience* . . . (Boston, 1744), in Edmund S.
Morgan, ed., *Puritan Political Ideas, 1558–1794* (Indianapolis, 1965), 304.

75. Storing, ed., *The Complete Anti-Federalist*, 6:229.

76. Warren, *History of the Rise, Progress and Termination of the American Revolution*
. . . (Boston, 1805), 3:364, 365.

77. On June 8, 1789, James Madison warned the first Congress that the desire for

"the lawgivers of the Union" had been equally distinguished for their patriotism and enlightenment: "They had all grown up at a time of social crisis, when the spirit of liberty had been in constant conflict with a strong and dominating authority."[78]

Although Sir Isaiah Berlin has assured us that late in the eighteenth century Immanuel Kant achieved a philosophical reconciliation of liberty and authority—literally made them coincide and therefore cease to be in tension—that message does not seem to have carried over into nineteenth- and twentieth-century America. John C. Calhoun would regard the relationship between liberty and authority as *the* great conundrum of government; and as recently as 1954 Justice Robert H. Jackson reflected that "perhaps the most delicate, difficult and shifting of all balances which the Court is expected to maintain is that between liberty and authority."[79]

Once ratification had been accomplished, Madison was prepared to fulfill his commitment to achieving passage of a bill of rights. Although he genuinely believed that such a precaution might be useful, he seems to have been skeptical of its necessity, and for two reasons: first because he felt that government in the United States would somehow be different, would function in a manner for which no precedents existed; but second because he did not think that historical experience supplied sufficient guidelines. His ruminations on this topic to Thomas Jefferson are fascinating:

> Perhaps too there may be a certain degree of danger, that a succession of artful and ambitious rulers, may by gradual and well-timed advances, finally

---

a Bill of Rights was very strong. He referred to "the jealousy they have for their liberty" and the demands that provision be made for "those securities for liberty." He also pointed out that the Antifederalists themselves saw the state legislature as "sure guardians of the people's liberty." Smith and Murphy, eds., *Liberty and Justice*, 80–82.

78. Tocqueville, *Democracy in America*, edited by J. P. Mayer (Anchor ed.: Garden City, NY, 1969), 152.

79. Berlin, *Two Concepts of Liberty* (Oxford, 1958), 33; August O. Spain, *The Political Theory of John C. Calhoun* (New York, 1968), ch. 4; Jackson, *The Supreme Court in the American System of Government* (Cambridge, MA, 1955), 75. See also J. Allen Smith, *The Growth and Decadence of Constitutional Government* (New York, 1930), ch. 14, "Individual Liberty and Governmental Authority."

erect an independent Government on the subversion of liberty. Should this danger exist at all, it is prudent to guard against it, especially when the precaution can do no injury. At the same time I must own that I see no tendency in our governments to danger on that side. It has been remarked that there is a tendency in all Governments to an augmentation of power at the expence of liberty. But the remark as usually understood does not appear to me well founded. Power when it has attained a certain degree of energy and independence goes on generally to further degrees. But when below that degree, the direct tendency is to further degrees of relaxation, until the abuses of liberty beget a sudden transition to an undue degree of power. With this explanation the remark may be true; and in the latter sense only is it in my opinion applicable to the Governments in America. It is a melancholy reflection that liberty should be equally exposed to danger whether the Government have too much or too little power; and that the line which divides these extremes should be so inaccurately defined by experience.[80]

Madison's realistic view of human weakness combined with his concern for institutional controls caused him to sound, at times, remarkably like John Winthrop in his 1645 speech "On Liberty." Madison's discussion in *Federalist* number 37 of the fallibility of lawmakers seems to echo Winthrop on the same point. Similarly, when John Jay spoke at the very first Circuit Court, held in New York on April 4, 1790, his definition of civil liberty does not sound so far removed from Winthrop's, except that the context of his charge has become entirely secular:

It cannot be too strongly impressed on the minds of all how greatly our individual prosperity depends on our National prosperity, and how greatly our National prosperity depends on a well-organized, vigorous government, ruling by wise and equal laws, faithfully executed. Nor is such a government unfriendly to liberty—that liberty which is really estimable. On the contrary, nothing but a strong government of laws, irresistibly bearing down arbitrary power and licentiousness, can defend it against those two formidable enemies. Let it be remembered that civil liberty consists, not in a right to every man to do just what he pleases, but it consists in an equal right to all citizens to have, enjoy and do, in peace, security and without molestation, what-

80. Madison to Jefferson, October 17, 1788, Boyd, ed., *Papers of Thomas Jefferson*, 14:20.

ever the equal and constitutional laws of the country admit to be consistent with the public good.[81]

If the founders did not reconcile liberty and authority as exquisitely in practice as Kant had done in theory, Jay's lucid statement in 1790 at least indicates that an approximate consensus had been achieved as the new government came into existence. Problems of liberty and authority that would emerge in subsequent generations involved new sorts of issues and problems, such as the question that James Wilson called in 1787 "federal liberty," that is, just how much sovereignty (or authority) the states would have to surrender to the Union.[82]

Similarly, a reconciliation also took place in the traditional concern for liberty and property. Obviously, accommodation was much less difficult on this issue because many inhabitants of the Anglo-American world during the eighteenth century assumed the compatibility of these qualities. In 1796 William Plumer of New Hampshire would emphasize the importance of the Supreme Court because there, above all, "questions of the greatest magnitude, not only as regard the National character, but the lives, liberty and property of individuals must ultimately be decided." In 1829 Justice Joseph Story indicated that "the Rights of personal liberty and private property" ought to be held sacred. *Pro forma* statements of that sort would continue to appear.[83]

81. Cooke, ed., *The Federalist*, 232–33; Jay is quoted in Warren, *Supreme Court in United States History*, 1:60. For a succinct discussion of the varied contexts and meanings of liberty in the later eighteenth century, see Joyce Appleby, *Capitalism and a New Social Order: The Republican Vision of the 1790s* (New York, 1984), 15–22.

82. McCloskey, ed., *Works of James Wilson*, 2:767–68. See also ibid., 647.

83. Plumer to Jeremiah Smith, March 31, 1796, quoted in Warren, *Supreme Court in United States History*, 1:140–41; Story is quoted in Edward S. Corwin, *Liberty Against Government: The Rise, Flowering and Decline of a Famous Juridical Concept* (Baton Rouge, 1948), 67; Charles Evans Hughes, *Addresses and Papers* (New York, 1908), 139; Warren, *Supreme Court in United States History*, 3:477, quoting George W. Wickersham in 1912.

There is, however, a highly significant complication: namely, the continuation of chattel slavery between 1787 and 1865, which needless to say created all manner of conflict over liberty and property. It has been argued that in the minds of the founders, property was *the* fundamental liberty, and that neither the Fifth nor the Fourteenth Amendment made any distinction between liberty and property.[84] Although that statement is true as far as it goes, it is incomplete from a historical point of view. Numerous invocations of liberty and property prior to the Civil War were made precisely with reference to slavery and to the Federal government's obligation to protect the institution where it existed and to assist slaveowners in recapturing those fugitives who preferred to be property no longer. How refreshing it is, therefore, to notice the ironic turn in Andrew Johnson's first annual message to Congress, dated December 4, 1865, where he insisted that "good faith requires the security of the freedmen in their liberty and their property, their right to labor, and their right to claim the just return of their labor."[85]

All too soon, by the early 1880s, the relationship between liberty and property would begin to undergo an extraordinary transformation, at least in legal and constitutional terms. Long before that, however, starting in the 1790s, public discourse on the subject of liberty in the United States moved in a new and highly symptomatic direction. References to liberty and authority, to civil liberty, and to political liberty by no means vanished; but the nineteenth century's obsession was destined to be liberty and order.

---

84. Berger, *Government by Judiciary*, 267.

85. See Franklin Pierce, fourth annual message to Congress, December 2, 1856, in Richardson, ed., *Messages and Papers of the Presidents*, 5:401. For Johnson, ibid., 6:360. In a proclamation dated September 3, 1867, Johnson stressed "the protection of the lives, liberty, property, and happiness of the people." Ibid., 546.

1. "Liberty & Property Without Any New Excise," tin-glazed earthenware bowl, English (ca. 1740–50). (Courtesy, The Henry Francis du Pont Museum, Winterthur, DE.)

2. Liberty signboard from the Bissell Tavern, Bissell's Ferry, East Windsor, Connecticut. Wood and wrought iron. Originally made in 1777; repainted in 1781 and 1801. (Courtesy, National Gallery of Art, Washington, D.C.)

3. "Liberty Displaying the Arts and Sciences," oil on linen by Samuel Jennings (1792). Beneath the lyre are sheets of music on which the words and notes of George Frederick Handel's air, "Come, Ever-smiling Liberty," from *Judas Maccabaeus* (1747) are inscribed. "Cato's Letters," number 67 (February 24, 1721), was entitled "Arts and Sciences the Effects of Civil Liberty only, and ever destroyed or oppressed by Tyranny." In 1776 Richard Price wrote that "Liberty is the soil where the arts and sciences have flourished." (Courtesy, The Henry Francis du Pont Museum, Winterthur, DE.)

4. Liberty and the American eagle, elaborate silk embroidery on silk (ca. 1788–1800). This unique work may have been a processional banner made for a special occasion, such as an inaugural parade, or else for presentation to someone of considerable stature, such as George Washington. Note the crown, serpent, and chains beneath Miss Liberty's feet. (Courtesy, The National Museum of American History, Smithsonian Institution, Washington, D.C.)

5. Liberty, an anonymous naive (or primitive) painting on canvas (ca. 1803–11). An adaptation of the popular painting and engraving by Edward Savage: "Liberty, in the form of the Goddess of Youth, giving support to the Bald Eagle" (Philadelphia, 1796). (Courtesy, National Gallery of Art [Garbisch Collection], Washington, D.C.)

6. Liberty with cornucopia, painted silk (ca. 1800–1825). The painted floral border is edged on both sides with silver-colored purl and spangles. Purl is a coiled wire that is stitched onto the surface of a fabric. The picture is believed to have been made at Abby Wright's school in South Hadley, Massachusetts. The cornucopia was symbolic of abundance and prosperity in the young republic. (Courtesy, Division of Textiles, National Museum of American History, Smithsonian Institution, Washington, D.C.)

7. Liberty, anonymous silk needlework on silk and paint (ca. 1820–40). Another rendition of the influential Edward Savage painting and engraving. (Courtesy, Birmingham Museum of Art, Birmingham, AL.)

8. Liberty coverlet, navy blue and white jacquard wool, woven in Ithaca, New York, by Archibald Davidson for Phebe Robertson (1832). The coverlet is reversible, and "Liberty" is repeated around all four borders. (Courtesy, Hinckley Foundation Museum, Ithaca, NY.)

9. Liberty coverlet with an eagle design, dark red and cream (ca. 1845), using a tied, double-weave or "Biderwind" technique. (Courtesy, Cortland County Historical Society, Inc., Cortland, NY.)

10. Liberty crowning George Washington, painted on a fire pumper built in New York City (ca. 1832), initially used there and subsequently in Oxford, New York. (Courtesy, Adirondack Museum, Blue Mountain Lake, NY.)

11. Tan clay pitcher with a blue transfer print, made during the later 1830s as a memorial to Elijah Lovejoy, the abolitionist printer who was killed by a mob at Alton, Illinois, on November 7, 1837. On the opposite side a cartouche with a sunburst background contains all the words of the First Amendment to the U.S. Constitution. On the side shown, Liberty stands beside a printing press, and a slave kneels at her side. (Courtesy, Hinckley Foundation Museum, Ithaca, NY.)

12. Liberty flask made by the Willington Glass Company, West Willington, Connecticut (ca. 1850–60). (Courtesy, Hinckley Foundation Museum, Ithaca, NY.)

Part Two

*

Ordered Liberty and Law in Nineteenth-Century America

"American liberty is not a mystical, undefined liberty; it is a practical liberty, in harmony with the peculiar genius of the people and its peculiar destiny; it is a liberty of action and motion which the American uses to expand over the vast territory that Providence has given him and to subdue it to his uses."

Michel Chevalier, *Society, Manners and Politics in the United States; Being a series of Letters on North America* (Paris, 1836; Boston, 1839).

"Our inheritance is an inheritance of American liberty. That liberty is characteristic, peculiar, and altogether our own. Nothing like it existed in former times. . . . With us its principles have become interwoven into the minds of individual men, connected with our daily opinions and our daily habits, until it is, if I may say so, an element of social as well as of political life; and the consequence is, that to whatever region an American citizen carries himself, he takes with him, fully developed in his own understanding and experience, our American principles and opinions, and becomes ready at once, in co-operation with others, to apply them to the formation of new governments."

Daniel Webster, "An address at the laying of the Corner-stone of the Addition to the Capitol, on the 4th of July, 1851."

Theodore Dwight, a Connecticut lawyer and political journalist, observed in 1794 that liberty was much valued and widely discussed as the new nation sought to find its way and establish an identity. "At the present period," he noted, "when the principles of liberty are so highly revered, and the practice of them so justly admired, every question, in which they are involved, ought to be discussed by the soundest reason, and established on the most substantial justice."[1]

Liberty was talked about extensively, to be sure, especially in relation to republicanism and the new Constitution. Having made a Revolution in the name of liberty, and having established a new system of government that many people believed to be without precedent, Americans felt intense interest in the nature of liberty under this republican regime. How would it be used? Was it likely to be abused? Was it fully compatible with republicanism? And if so, would the combination of the two make the United States distinctive in the annals of political society? David Ramsay epitomized the mood that so many people felt during the post-revolutionary generation: "The adoption of this constitution was a triumph of virtue and good sense, over the vices and follies of human nature. In some respects, the merit of it is greater than that of the declaration of independence. . . . The instances of nations, which had vindicated their liberty by the sword, are many; of those which made a good use of their liberty when acquired, are comparatively few."[2]

New formulations and linkages concerning the concept of liberty appeared, though most of them are more properly categorized as "climate of opinion" slogans than as contributions to the history of political thought. Predictably, perhaps, "liberty and independence"

1. Dwight, "An Oration, Spoken Before the Connecticut Society, for the Promotion of Freedom and the Relief of Persons Unlawfully Holden in Bondage" (Hartford, 1794), in Charles S. Hyneman and Donald S. Lutz, eds., *American Political Writing during the Founding Era, 1760–1805* (Indianapolis, 1983), 2:894.

2. Ramsay, *Universal History; or, An Historical View of Asia, Africa, Europe, and America . . .* (Philadelphia, 1818), 3:53.

became a favorite in public discourse from the 1790s until the 1830s;[3] just as "liberty and union" enjoyed considerable popularity from the time of the Nullification Crisis early in the 1830s through the conclusion of the Civil War.[4] Liberty and equality, liberty and peace, even liberty and Protestantism (part of the anti-French and anti-Spanish mood that accompanied the explorations of Lewis and Clark) were invoked, though much less commonly.[5]

Some familiar phrases also lingered on—particularly the well-established distinction between natural and civil liberty and the standard usage of liberty and property—though without much innovation or even thoughtful adaptation to changing circumstances. Perhaps the most noteworthy new application of conventional terms in the nineteenth-century cultural context took the form of national zealousness, a missionary call to proselytize on behalf of American liberty.[6] As for "political liberty," its hey-day had apparently passed—at least, many moderates and conservatives hoped that it had. (Jeffersonians and Jacksonians, to be sure, would harbor different hopes.) In 1798 William Cobbett was dismissed as physician to the Philadelphia Dispensary on the grounds that he was "a friend to political liberty."[7]

3. See John Adams's address to the Senate, December 11, 1798, in James D. Richardson, ed., *A Compilation of the Messages and Papers of the Presidents, 1789–1897* (Washington, D.C., 1896–99), 1:276; Fisher Ames, "Laocoon II" (*Boston Gazette*, April 1799), in Seth Ames, ed., *The Life and Works of Fisher Ames* (Boston, 1854), 2:127. The Winterthur Museum in Delaware owns a coverlet, made in Ithaca, New York (1834), with the motto "Liberty & Independence" woven into one corner.

4. Henry Clay (1832), for example, is quoted in Sacvan Bercovitch, *The American Jeremiad* (Madison, 1978), 150.

5. See James M. Lindgren, "The Gospel of Preservation in Virginia and New England: Historic Preservation and the Regeneration of Traditionalism" (unpub. Ph.D. dissertation, College of William and Mary, 1984), 186. The municipal seal of Milledgeville, Georgia (once the state capital), includes an angel holding a banner emblazoned with two words: "Liberty" and "Christianity."

6. See the charge presented in 1803 by Justice Samuel Chase, in Alan F. Westin, ed., *An Autobiography of the Supreme Court: Off-the-Bench Commentary by the Justices* (New York, 1963), 69–70; and see Isaac F. Shepard, "Liberty and Its Mission: An Oration, delivered before the citizens of West Killingley, Conn., July 4, 1856" (Boston, 1856), 11–16.

7. Quoted in Richard J. Twomey, "Jacobins and Jeffersonians: Anglo-American Radi-

The predominant usage swiftly became "liberty with order," often lauded as "ordered liberty." It flourished as a ubiquitous call—after a while a kind of conditioned response—ranging from New England to the South, from George Washington down to Herbert Hoover, from pulpits to utterly secular rostrums, and from one political party to the next. On New Year's Day, 1795, George Washington issued a proclamation setting aside February 19 as a day of public thanksgiving, "particularly for the possession of constitutions of government which unite and by their union establish liberty with order."[8] The generation of Daniel Webster and Martin Van Buren invoked that phrase repeatedly,[9] as did Abraham Lincoln and his contemporaries throughout the crisis of the Civil War. A European emigré like Francis Lieber, who eventually migrated from South Carolina to New York, did not equate liberty with equality or democracy; he insisted upon liberty and order. And in 1861, while preparing a bill of rights for the new constitution of Georgia, Thomas R. R. Cobb declared that "good order in society is essential to true liberty."[10]

What these phrases really meant to the public mind becomes clearer in the context of several statements made near the turn of the century. The Reverend Jeremiah Atwater, for example, offered a sermon in 1801 to the governor and legislature of Vermont, two years before he was chosen the first president of Middlebury College. Atwater proceeded very deliberately, but the essence of his argument can be extracted.

---

cal Ideology, 1790–1810," in Margaret and James Jacob, eds., *The Origins of Anglo-American Radicalism* (London, 1984), 294.

8. Washington's proclamation appears in Richardson, ed., *Messages and Papers of the Presidents*, 1:180. For similar invocations at the time by John Adams, David Tappan, and others, see Bercovitch, *American Jeremiad*, 135–38, 149.

9. For Webster see Robert A. Ferguson, *Law and Letters in American Culture* (Cambridge, MA, 1984), 212, 232; for Van Buren see his inaugural address, March 4, 1837, in Richardson, ed., *Messages and Papers of the Presidents*, 3:316.

10. See Lincoln's proclamation of August 12, 1861, in Richardson, ed., *Messages and Papers of the Presidents*, 6:36; for Lieber see Phillip S. Paludan, *A Covenant with Death: The Constitution, Law, and Equality in the Civil War Era* (Urbana, 1975), 69–75, 101; and

Liberty is a sound dear to us all: But what do we understand by it? One, perhaps, denotes by it, a license to do what he pleases and considers every kind and degree of restraint, as tyranny, whether that restraint originates with the individual himself, or is imposed by civil rulers. . . . Liberty, if considered as a blessing, must be taken in a qualified sense. The freedom which it implies, must be a limited, not absolute freedom. . . . [Unbounded liberty] would arm the idle and profligate against the virtuous and industrious, and instead of a rational liberty, would be seen and felt to be, the worst of tyrannies. . . . To restrain such an absurd liberty, government was instituted. Restraint, in some degree or other, is its very object: And to exclaim in favor of liberty as wholly opposite to restraint, is to oppose the very end for which government itself is instituted.[11]

An anonymous Boston essayist expressed the outlook of thousands in 1804: "Where there is no law there is no liberty"; and yet another writer combined these two assertions in a declaration that enjoyed wide approval:

Real liberty is not the power of doing what we please, but is a system of RESTRAINT, by which we are PREVENTED from injuring another in property or person, and are in like manner ourselves protected from his violence and injustice. Real liberty is a code of laws. . . . Real liberty has for her officiating minister, judges, sheriffs and constables, whilst her residence is surrounded by gaols, pillories, and gibbets.[12]

If that seems to have a rather extreme ring, rest assured that most judges and lawyers fully sympathized even though they may have used less fanatical language. They characteristically pleaded

---

for Cobb see William B. McCash, *Thomas R. R. Cobb (1823–1862): The Making of a Southern Nationalist* (Macon, GA, 1983), 229.

11.   Atwater, "A Sermon" (Middlebury, VT, 1801), in Hyneman and Lutz, eds., *American Political Writing during the Founding Era*, 2:1172. For context see Charles A. Barker, ed., *Power and Law: American Dilemma in World Affairs* (Baltimore, 1971), esp. the essays by Charles E. Rosenberg, "Anxiety, Ideology, and Order: Reflections on the Making of American Public Policy," and William L. Neumann, "Law and Order in American Thought: An Ambiguous Heritage," 22–33 and 55–65.

12.   From *The Repertory* (Boston), August 10, 1804, and December 18, 1804, both quoted in Richard E. Ellis, *The Jeffersonian Crisis: Courts and Politics in the Young Republic* (New York, 1971), 204–5.

for "liberty without anarchy." Nathan Dane hoped the new nation would achieve a wise "union of law and liberty." In 1812 Justice Joseph Story perceived liberty as the enemy of order; and in 1835, when his beloved colleague died, Story insisted that John Marshall had understood better than any other contemporary the vital balance between liberty and order.[13]

Some aspects of these statements and expressions of concern strike a familiar note, and understandably so. Almost half a century ago C. H. McIlwain reminded us that a dialogue between liberty and order was noticeable in medieval thought. Roger Williams had wrestled with the problem of achieving a proper distribution of the two in Rhode Island during the midseventeenth century.[14] And late in the nineteenth century Woodrow Wilson acknowledged the longevity of the larger issue:

> We know that the history of politics has been the history of liberty; a history of the enlargement of the sphere of independent individual action at the expense of the sphere of dictatorial authority. It has revealed a process of differentiation. Certain freedoms of opinion and utterance, of choice of occupation and of allegiance, of fair trial and equitable condemnation, have been blocked out as inviolable territories, lying quite beyond the jurisdiction of political sovereignty. Beginning with that singular and interesting order of the classical states of the ancient world, under which the individual was merged in the community and liberty became identical with a share in the exercise of the public power, we witness something like a gradual disintegration, a resolution of the State into its constituent elements, until at length those who govern and those who are governed are no longer one and the same, but stand face to face treating with one another, agreeing upon terms

13. For Alexander Dallas's concern with liberty and order in Pennsylvania, see Ellis, *The Jeffersonian Crisis*, 171, 180 (both examples from 1805); for Dane see Elizabeth Kelley Bauer, *Commentaries on the Constitution, 1790–1860* (New York, 1952), 131; and see R. Kent Newmyer, *Supreme Court Justice Joseph Story: Statesman of the Old Republic* (Chapel Hill, 1985), 86–87, 196.

14. McIlwain, *Constitutionalism Ancient and Modern* (Ithaca, 1947), 136–37; Theodore Dwight Bozeman, "Religious Liberty and the Problem of Order in Early Rhode Island," *New England Quarterly* 45 (March 1972): 63–64; Roger Williams to the Townsmen of Providence, January 1655, in Paul M. Angle, ed., *By These Words . . .* (Chicago, 1954), 36–37.

of command and obedience, as at Runnymede. Conditions of submission have been contested, and, as liberty has gained upon authority, have been jealously formulated. The procedure and the prerogatives of authority have been agreed upon; liberty has encroached upon sovereignty and set bounds to it. The process is old; only some of its results are new.[15]

What is so striking about the emergence of this theme in nineteenth-century America, however, is its pervasiveness, its persistence, the intensity with which it was felt, and the multiplicity as well as the simultaneity of stimuli underlying it. We must not forget the fear of political anarchy, an anxiety that lingered long after Shays's Rebellion had finally been suppressed in 1787, an anxiety that prompted Joel Barlow to devote one substantial section of an 1801 pamphlet to "the means of securing interior liberty in the United States."[16]

In addition, and closely related, there was a dread that something remotely comparable to the French Revolution, with its social levelling and chaos, might occur in the United States; and that our peaceful Revolution to achieve limited ends might be tainted by the domestic violence of theirs. Edward Everett expressed a commonly heard derision in his 1828 Fourth of July oration entitled "The History of Liberty": "Hence the dreadful excesses that marked the progress of the French Revolution, and, for a while, almost made the name of liberty odious."[17]

Many people worried that the radical rhetoric and political val-

15. Wilson, *An Old Master, and Other Political Essays* (New York, 1893), 83–84. For a valuable exploration of the meaning of order in seventeenth-century England, see Keith Wrightson, "Two Concepts of Order: Justices, Constables and Jurymen in Seventeenth-Century England," in John Brewer and John Styles, eds., *An Ungovernable People: The English and Their Law in the Seventeenth and Eighteenth Centuries* (New Brunswick, NJ, 1980), 21–46, esp. 24.

16. Barlow, "To His Fellow Citizens of the United States. Letter II: On Certain Political Measures Proposed to Their Consideration" (Philadelphia, 1801), in Hyneman and Lutz, eds., *American Political Writing during the Founding Era*, 2:1113–25.

17. Everett, "The History of Liberty," an oration delivered at Charlestown, Massachusetts, July 4, 1828, in Everett, *Orations and Speeches on Various Occasions* (9th ed.: Boston, 1878), 1:167. See also George M. Fredrickson, *White Supremacy: A Comparative Study in American and South African History* (New York, 1981), 147.

ues of 1776 would continue to be persuasive, even contagious, long after their "moment" of nationalistic usefulness had passed. "A democracy cannot last," wrote Fisher Ames in 1805. "Its nature ordains, that its next change shall be into a military despotism. . . . The reason is, that the tyranny of what is called the people, and that by the sword, both operate alike to debase and corrupt, till there are neither men left with the spirit to desire liberty, nor morals with the power to sustain justice."[18]

Others with a pessimistic view of human nature—and there were many by the 1790s—shared the concern voiced by Chief Justice Thomas McKean of Pennsylvania: "Who is there to control the wanton passions of men, suddenly raised to power and frisking in the pasture of true liberty, yet not sufficiently secured by proper barriers?"[19] Precisely because human nature was cautiously regarded, and the "passions" were so mistrusted, an obsessive concern started to spread that liberty might degenerate into "licentiousness," perhaps the most frequently used pejorative phrase of the late eighteenth and early nineteenth centuries. Speaking on the Fourth of July in 1788, James Wilson labelled licentiousness the enemy of liberty. George Washington warned in his first inaugural address that Americans would need "to discriminate the spirit of liberty from that of licentiousness," a caution that he repeated in 1794. Perez Fobes of Rhode Island feared that an excess of liberty would inevitably lead to licentiousness, and he made that the burden of an election sermon in 1795—a theme echoed by Fisher Ames a decade later. John Trumbull popularized the point in his mock epic "M'Fingal" (1782), suggesting that a sense of proportion and respect for law had been dissipated as the Revolution progressed.[20]

---

18. Ames, "The Dangers of American Liberty" (Boston, 1805), in Hyneman and Lutz, eds., *American Political Writing during the Founding Era*, 2:1332.

19. Quoted in Henry Adams, *The Life of Albert Gallatin* (Philadelphia, 1879), 313.

20. Wilson, "Oration Delivered on the Fourth of July 1788, at the Procession Formed at Philadelphia to Celebrate the Adoption of the Constitution of the United States," in Robert G. McCloskey, ed., *The Works of James Wilson* (Cambridge, MA, 1967), 2:777–78; Richardson, ed., *Messages and Papers of the Presidents*, 1:66, 166; Hyneman and Lutz, eds.,

Consequently the catchphrase "liberty and order" would not have seemed a paradoxical oxymoron to Americans of that era. Combining the two qualities was an ideal way to achieve a golden mean between anarchy and despotism. In a textbook on American law published in 1837, Timothy Walker worded the issue in language for laymen: "From the commencement of civilization, the grand problem in politics has been, to attain the exact medium between anarchy on the one hand, and despotism on the other. . . . Of course the fair conclusion is, that we enjoy that golden mean so long looked for, but never before discovered."[21]

Practical considerations also prompted this quest for order. Advocates of commercial growth wanted the kind of political and social stability that would facilitate economic expansion with as few ups and downs as possible. J. Willard Hurst has persuasively explained that public policy during the early nineteenth century supported the positive use of law to shape the social environment and provide a viable balance of power that could enhance opportunities for organized groups as well as private individuals. Businessmen, boosters, and legislators tended to emphasize two vital elements in achieving a new degree of liberty: the release of man's innate skills and energies alongside an increase in available entrepreneurial options.[22] Daniel Webster particularized the linkage in 1834 when he remarked that "the history of banks belongs to the history of commerce and the general history of liberty."[23]

American Political Writing during the Founding Era, 2:1001, 1304; Ferguson, *Law and Letters in American Culture*, 107–9.

21. Quoted in Perry Miller, *The Life of the Mind in America from the Revolution to the Civil War* (New York, 1965), 218. For evidence of widespread support at this time for a society based upon liberty and order, see David J. Rothman, *The Discovery of the Asylum: Social Order and Disorder in the New Republic* (Boston, 1971), and Howard Marraro, *American Opinion on the Unification of Italy, 1846–1861* (New York, 1932), 308.

22. See Ralph Lerner, "Commerce and Character: The Anglo-American as New-Model Man," *William and Mary Quarterly* 36 (January 1979): 4; Hurst, *Law and the Conditions of Freedom in the Nineteenth-Century United States* (Madison, 1956), 37, 43.

23. Quoted in Maurice G. Baxter, *One and Inseparable: Daniel Webster and the Union* (Cambridge, MA, 1984), 233.

Another practical consideration developed from the realities of human migration westward, a phenomenon that accelerated during the later 1780s and never let up throughout the nineteenth century. Philip Freneau embodied an enduring ideal in his poem called "On the emigration to America, and peopling the western Country," published in 1787 in the first issue of *The American Museum*:

> Here reason shall new laws devise
> And order from confusion rise.

When Manasseh Cutler supervised new settlements in Ohio early in the century, he explicitly insisted upon the need for social order and proper subordination. Like Webster, his fellow New Englander, Cutler regarded the acceptance of political and social deference as a necessary basis for the achievement of ordered liberty.[24]

By comparison with unruly western frontiers, the settled seaboard and its established institutions looked like a paragon of what the nation as a whole should aspire to. No one knew that better than Aaron Burr, whose flamboyant career made him familiar with the West as well as the East. In Vice President Burr's farewell address to the Senate (November 1804), he commented that "this house is a sanctuary; a citadel of law, of order, and of liberty."[25]

Was the problem of disorder genuine, imagined, or overblown? Did it warrant the anxiety that John Adams conveyed to Jefferson in 1813: "When? Where? and how? is the present Chaos to be arranged into order?" The problem seemed fundamentally real to the founders because they had to cope with factionalism, which they regarded simultaneously as a phenomenon that liberty "nourished,"

---

24. Ferguson, *Law and Letters in American Culture*, 251.

25. Matthew L. Davis, *Memoirs of Aaron Burr, with Miscellaneous Selections from His Correspondence* (New York, 1836–37), 2:362.

yet one that also fostered political disorder. Fisher Ames phrased it as a formula in 1805: that "liberty is lost where faction domineers; that some security must be provided against its attacks; and that no elective government can be secure or orderly, unless it be invested by the Constitution itself with the means of self-defence."[26]

Nagging doubts about factionalism fit into a larger issue that had vexed American statesmen throughout the final quarter of the eighteenth century: Might the republican mode of government be incompatible with the maintenance of civil liberty? Precisely because historical examples seemed to require an affirmative answer, Madison and Hamilton felt a special obligation in writing *The Federalist Papers* to explain why the American case could be different. Hamilton articulated the dilemma along with his response early on in *Federalist* number 9:

> From the disorders that disfigure the annals of those republics, the advocates of despotism have drawn arguments, not only against the forms of republican government, but against the very principles of civil liberty. They have decried all free government, as inconsistent with the order of society, and have indulged themselves in malicious exultation over its friends and partizans. Happily for mankind, stupendous fabrics reared on the basis of liberty, which have flourished for ages, have in a few glorious instances refuted their gloomy sophisms. And, I trust, America will be the broad and solid foundation of other edifices not less magnificent, which will be equally permanent monuments of their errors.[27]

Madison addressed several facets of the problem through his contributions as "Publius." In number 37 he acknowledged that "the genius of Republican liberty, seems to demand on one side, not only that all power should be derived from the people; but, that those entrusted with it should be kept in dependence on the people. . . ." In number 63, however, after scrutinizing republicanism in ancient times, Madison conceded that although such failed

26. Adams to Jefferson, July 15, 1813, in Lester J. Cappon, ed., *The Adams-Jefferson Letters* (Chapel Hill, 1959), 2:358; Ames, "The Dangers of American Liberty" in Hyneman and Lutz, eds., *American Political Writing during the Founding Era*, 2:1319.

27. Jacob E. Cooke, ed., *The Federalist* (Middletown, CT, 1961), 51.

examples "are repugnant to the genius of America," they nonetheless provided "very instructive proofs of the necessity of some institution that will blend stability with liberty."[28]

Madison answered the most critical issue of all in *Federalist* number 10, and he did so in epigrammatic language: "Liberty is to faction, what air is to fire, an aliment without which it instantly expires." He then supplied an appropriate response: "But it could not be a less folly to abolish liberty, which is essential to political life, [just] because it nourishes faction, than it would be to wish the annihilation of air, which is essential to animal life, because it imparts to fire its destructive agency."[29]

In numbers 45 and 55 Madison moved to the specific grounds for his optimism concerning the healthy interaction between liberty, faction, and order in the United States. In number 45 (and elsewhere) he looked to the Constitution itself, along with its carefully calibrated institutional checks, as being "essential to guard them [the American people] against those violent and oppressive factions which embitter the blessings of liberty." In number 55 he revealed his own judicious assessment of human nature—less naively optimistic than Jefferson's, yet less cynical than John Adams's as well:

No offices therefore can be dealt out to the existing members, but such as may become vacant by ordinary casualties; and to suppose that these would be sufficient to purchase [i.e., corrupt] the guardians of the people, selected by the people themselves, is to renounce every rule by which events ought to be calculated, and to substitute an indiscriminate and unbounded jealousy, with which all reasoning must be vain. The sincere friends of liberty who give themselves up to the extravagancies of this passion are not aware of the injury they do their own cause. As there is a degree of depravity in mankind which requires a certain degree of circumspection and distrust: So there are other qualities in human nature, which justify a certain portion of esteem and confidence. Republican government presupposes the existence of these qualities in a higher degree than any other form.[30]

28. Ibid., 234, 426. See also *Federalist* number 52.
29. Cooke, ed., *The Federalist*, 58.
30. Ibid., 308, 377–78.

Although Montesquieu may have been the most influential political philosopher for the framers in 1787–88, they differed from him in one very major respect. Not only did Montesquieu decline to associate liberty with any particular form of government (see *The Spirit of the Laws*, Book XI, chapter 4), he believed that republics were most likely to be plagued by faction and that, consequently, liberty was no more secure in a republic than under a monarchy. By contrast, Americans associated liberty with republican government in general and with the version of it that they had devised in particular. Alexander Hamilton made that argument in *Federalists* 70, 85, and elsewhere.[31] Even before Americans began to regard themselves as "Nature's Nation," therefore, they had surely emerged as Liberty's Republic.

The degree of consensus on that point is truly remarkable, and the limited range of deviation from it quite striking. We might very well expect a conservative like Fisher Ames to have identified himself with "the friends of order and true liberty" (in a letter to Alexander Hamilton dated August 26, 1800). Back in 1789 Ames had established a position that he would embellish at every subsequent opportunity:

> I am commonly opposed to those who modestly assume the rank of champions of liberty, and make a very patriotic noise about the people. . . . I love liberty as well as anybody. I am proud of it, as the true title of our people to distinction above others. . . . But I would guard it by making the laws strong enough to protect it.[32]

Over and over again Ames would refer, in public essays as well as in private correspondence, to "the good old cause of order, law, and liberty," to the sacredness of "liberty and property," and to the essential need to champion ordered liberty at the expense of anything resembling "natural liberty," the lamentable type of liberty that was "the tendency of revolution itself."[33]

31. Ibid., 471, 588. See also Abraham Lincoln's General Orders, number 16, February 18, 1862, in Richardson, ed., *Messages and Papers of the Presidents*, 6:106.
32. Ames, ed., *Life and Works of Fisher Ames*, 1:280, 56; 2:5.
33. Ibid., 2:143, 127, 293, 298; 1:310.

Surely Thomas Jefferson, among all the contemporaries of Fisher Ames, was situated at the opposite end of the ideological spectrum. Contemporaries made that assumption about young Jefferson; and prior to his presidency, perhaps, their assessment was correct.[34] Jefferson in power, however, could be conciliatory and politic. In his second inaugural address (March 4, 1805) he went out of his way to assure the opposition party "that our wish as well as theirs is that the public efforts may be directed honestly to the public good, that peace be cultivated, civil and religious liberty unassailed, law and order preserved, equality of rights maintained, and that state of property, equal or unequal, which results to every man from his own industry or that of his father's." In 1823, he expressed sentiments to a European correspondent that scarcely sound like Jefferson the revolutionary: "Possessing ourselves the combined blessings of liberty and order, we wish the same to other countries."[35]

It would be naive as well as irresponsible to suggest that Thomas Jefferson and Fisher Ames were somhow ideological brethren. Significant differences separated them, to be sure; but with respect to the concept of liberty, at least, their differences may have had more to do with means than with ends. Both of them hoped to achieve an orderly republican society. Whereas Jefferson and his followers would not jeopardize liberty and sought equilibrium between liberty and order, Ames and his like-minded contemporaries were willing to subordinate liberty to order if necessary. Edward Everett chose to call himself and his political allies "the friends of liberty," a seductive and high-minded phrase left over from the radical impulse of the later eighteenth century. In reality it was a misnomer because ordered liberty was not what the Anglo-American radicals

---

34. See Forrest McDonald, *Alexander Hamilton: A Biography* (New York, 1979), 241, 254–57, 263–83.

35. Richardson, ed., *Messages and Papers of the Presidents*, 1:381–82; Jefferson to A. Coray, October 31, 1823, in Andrew A. Lipscomb, ed., *The Writings of Thomas Jefferson* (Washington, D.C., 1903), 15:481.

had in mind. The *Richmond Enquirer* was on target in 1807 when it labelled the disciples of Hamilton and the Federalist Party "the Friends of Order."³⁶

The friends of order, broadly viewed, talked about three different modes—all closely related—of achieving their goals. The first, ceaselessly repeated throughout the nineteenth century, was "regulated liberty." That vague phrase meant more than just governmental regulation; it meant the imposition of self-control by individuals. As schoolchildren learned to sing:

> America! America! God mend thine ev'ry flaw,
> Confirm thy soul in self-control,
> Thy liberty in law.³⁷

The second rhetorical mode, obviously connected and invoked even more often, was "liberty and law," a phrase with which Jefferson and John Quincy Adams (sons of Virginia and Massachusetts, Republican and proto-Whig) were just as comfortable as Millard Fillmore and James Buchanan. Fillmore reacted to the resistance that Boston abolitionists presented in 1851 to recovery of an alleged fugitive slave with a message to the U.S. Senate in which this sentence appeared: "In a community distinguished for its love of order and respect for the laws, among a people whose sentiment is liberty and law, and not liberty without law nor above the law, such an outrage could only be the result of sudden violence, unhappily too much unprepared for to be successfully resisted."³⁸

This bond became increasingly pervasive and visible, from the Centennial celebration of the Constitution in 1887 (in the grand

---

36. Everett, "The History of Liberty," 169, 171; *Richmond Enquirer* quoted in Irving Brant, *Storm Over the Constitution* (Indianapolis, 1936), 56.

37. Howard Mumford Jones, *The Pursuit of Happiness*, (Ithaca, 1953), 38 (from the Supreme Court of Indiana, 1855); Charles Warren, *The Supreme Court in United States History* (Boston, 1922), 3:185 (from *The Nation*, 1867). Henry F. May makes the point about "America" in *The End of American Innocence: A Study of the First Years of Our Own Times, 1912–1917* (New York, 1959), 45.

38. See Richardson, ed., *Messages and Papers of the Presidents*, 1:456; 2:295; 5:80, 101, 180, 469.

parade held on September 15, 1887, the explicit theme of one float was "Liberty and the Law") through the glory years of Progressivism during Teddy Roosevelt's presidency. No other American politician, in fact, seems to have been so fond of this phrase as Roosevelt, who reiterated it constantly. At Lincoln, Nebraska, for example, in 1903: "The principles of order, of law, and of liberty under and through the law, need to be actuated by a spirit of genuine brotherhood, the spirit which regards one's neighbors' interests as well as one's own, and which thinks it a shame to impugn the rights of anyone else."[39]

The third imperative, so utterly appropriate for a self-consciously Protestant nation in which the evangelical impulse was rapidly expanding, involved a linkage between liberty and morality. Fisher Ames made the connection in 1800 as part of his eulogy of George Washington. Chancellor James Kent, who spent fourteen years on New York's highest court, regarded law as a means of achieving moral order and insisted that liberty could only be understood in accordance with moral order as the ultimate goal of society. This too would be a durable theme. Speaking at Bangor, Maine, in 1902, Theodore Roosevelt told an audience at the fairground there that "the permanence of liberty and democracy depends upon a majority of the people being steadfast in morality. . . ."[40]

What were the most effective ways to inculcate these values? From the pulpit, in speeches to voluntary associations, and through the public school as that institution gradually spread during the course of the nineteenth century. Educational reformers were in-

---

39. See Hampton L. Carson, ed., *History of the Celebration of the One Hundredth Anniversary of the Promulgation of the Constitution of the United States* (Philadelphia, 1889), 1:446; 2:22; a speech by Rev. Dr. R. R. Meredith celebrating the 268th anniversary of the Pilgrims' landing, *New York Times*, December 22, 1888, p. 2; John Marshall Harlan, "Our Duty to Respect Legislative Enactments" (1896), in Westin, ed., *An Autobiography of the Supreme Court*, 119; Alfred H. Lewis, ed., *A Compilation of the Messages and Speeches of Theodore Roosevelt, 1901–1905* (Washington, D.C., 1906), 1:187, 281, 384, 479.

40. Ames, ed., *Life and Works of Fisher Ames*, 2:82; Paul E. Johnson, *A Shopkeeper's Millennium: Society and Revivals in Rochester, New York, 1815–1837* (New York, 1978); Lewis, ed., *Messages and Speeches of Theodore Roosevelt*, 1:100.

variably advocates of good order who cited liberty even when their highest goal was really social control. An oration given in 1797 to the General Society of Mechanics in New York City ended with this peroration: "Behold! the era of GENERAL VIRTUE, LIBERTY, and HAPPINESS is at hand"; two sentences earlier, though, the speaker lavished praise upon his ultimate social objective: "order and fair liberty." A popular textbook on the *Science of Government*, widely used during the 1830s and 40s, redefined natural liberty as moral liberty, namely, "the permission which nature gives to all mankind of disposing of their persons and property in the manner they shall judge most consonant to their own happiness; on condition . . . that they do not abuse this liberty to the injury of other men; and that they practise towards others those moral duties which these laws enjoin."[41]

Regulated liberty, liberty and law, liberty and morality: they are not exactly interchangeable concepts, but they reinforced each other very powerfully as bulwarks of ordered liberty. All the pieces of a value system seemed to be in place so that American culture could be more free, more virtuous, and more manageable than any society ever before known in the annals of civilization.

The predilection for moral liberty leads us back once again to a major issue with which we dealt in Part One: namely, European parallels and the problem of American distinctiveness. At first glance the whole matter seems reasonably uncomplicated. Merle Curti has quite wisely shown us the extent to which John Locke was

41. George J. Warner, *Means for the Preservation of Public Liberty. An Oration Delivered in the New Dutch Church, on the Fourth of July, 1797* . . . (New York, 1797), 19; Andrew W. Young, *Introduction to the Science of Government . . . Designed for the Use of Families and Schools* (3rd ed.: Albany, 1839), 17–18; and see David Tyack and Elisabeth Hansot, *Managers of Virtue: Public School Leadership in America, 1820–1980* (New York, 1982), 25–26, 44; Christopher Lasch, *The Culture of Narcissism: American Life in an Age of Diminishing Expectations* (New York, 1978), 132–33, 137.

"America's Philosopher";[42] and it is easy to comprehend why a society with strong evangelical inclinations—which the United States surely had during the first half of the nineteenth century—would understand moral liberty as a Lockean notion, or as one fully compatible with Locke's ideas. Liberty is desirable, but order is essential. Man's foremost duty is the worship of God; and if mankind only fulfills that obligation, then society is bound to be orderly. Without society, men and women cannot survive to worship God. By this neatly sequential process of reasoning, a necessary process achieved an attractive goal: moral liberty. Praise be to God, and to John Locke too.

What snarls matters up, however (while making them more interesting as well), is that Locke was not the only source of this important message, and there is no reason to believe that Americans had an exclusive or perfectly connected cable to Locke. Edmund Burke offered a similar message in 1791: "Men are qualified for civil liberty in exact proportion to their own disposition to put moral chains on their own appetites. . . ." And Tocqueville said quite the same thing in 1835.[43]

The pattern of English roots and parallels extends well beyond the interdependence of liberty and morality. As the eighteenth century neared its close, conservative intellectuals in Great Britain suggested that public men should not expect to develop new ideas concerning liberty. The best that they could achieve, or should aspire to, would be a happy medium between liberty and order. Those who held this view, and they seem to have been in the majority, feared the radical assertion—that above all else the object of civil government was to secure total freedom for all men—and worried that it would undermine the established order. Conservative spokesmen contended that liberty might not be secure for anyone if all

42. Curti, "The Great Mr. Locke: America's Philosopher, 1783–1861," *Huntington Library Bulletin*, no. 11 (April 1937): 107–51.

43. Burke, "Letter to a Member of the National Assembly" (1791), in *The Works of . . . Edmund Burke* (Bohn ed.: London, 1900), 2:555; Tocqueville, *Democracy in America*, edited by J. P. Mayer (Anchor ed.: Garden City, NY, 1969), 17.

men shared equally in political power. Therefore liberty was contingent upon the existence of a stable social order and upon the rule of law, both of which could only be guaranteed by men of property.[44]

Once again, Edmund Burke provides an ideal litmus because he addressed these issues explicitly in private correspondence as well as published works. Late in 1789, for example, he revealed his initial response to the French Revolution in a very long letter to Charles-Jean-François Depont. Here is the most pertinent extract:

> Of all the loose Terms in the world Liberty is the most indefinite. Permit me then to continue our conversation, and to tell You what the freedom is that I love and that to which I think all men intitled. It is not solitary, unconnected, individual, selfish Liberty. As if every Man was to regulate the whole of his Conduct by his own will. The Liberty I mean is *social* freedom. It is that state of things in which Liberty is secured by the equality of Restraint; A Constitution of things in which the liberty of no one Man, and no body of Men and no Number of men can find Means to trespass on the liberty of any Person or any description of Persons in the Society. This kind of liberty is indeed but another name for Justice, ascertained by wise Laws, and secured by well constructed institutions. I am sure, that Liberty, so incorporated, and in a manner, identified, with justice, must be infinitely dear to every one, who is capable of conceiving what it is. But whenever a separation is made between Liberty and Justice, neither is, in my opinion, safe.[45]

Americans knew nothing of this letter, of course, and we must assume that similar negative reactions to the French Revolution developed spontaneously in the Anglo-American world.[46] By 1791–92, however, Burke was elaborating these ideas in published speeches

44. See H. T. Dickinson, *Liberty and Property: Political Ideology in Eighteenth-Century Britain* (New York, 1977), 305–6, 317.

45. Burke to Depont (November 1789), in Alfred Cobban and Robert A. Smith, eds., *The Correspondence of Edmund Burke* (Chicago, 1967), 6:42.

46. See Joel Barlow, "A Letter to the National Convention of France on the Defects in the Constitution of 1791" (New York, 1792) in Hyneman and Lutz, eds., *American Political Writing during the Founding Era*, 2:812–38; Ames, ed., *Life and Works of Fisher Ames*, 2:82; George Wm. Brown, *The Origin and Growth of Civil Liberty in Maryland* (Baltimore, 1850), 27.

and treatises. While some were memorably aphoristic—"Liberty too must be limited in order to be possessed"—others explored in a relentlessly systematic manner the requisite rationale for achieving a proper balance between liberty and order in Britain. This sentence from a speech given in 1792 is representative: "I go on this ground, that government, representing the society, has a general superintending control over all the actions, and over all the publicly propagated doctrines of men, without which it never could provide adequately for all the wants of society; but then it is to use this power with an equitable discretion, the only bond of sovereign authority."[47]

Burke's reflections on liberty in general, and on the French situation particularly, became known in the United States, along with the opinions of like-minded Britons as well as those of radicals. For more than a decade, for almost a generation, Americans did not make elaborate claims on behalf of their liberties. In so far as they connected liberty with republicanism, there seems to have been an assumption that the nature of civil liberty in the United States was indeed different. But the assumption tended to remain implicit rather than explicit; and it did not immediately serve as the basis for national chauvinism.

During the 1820s, however, that swiftly began to change. In the final segment of Book XI in *The Spirit of the Laws,* Montesquieu merely claimed to have described the potential for liberty under the English constitution, rather than the actual degree of liberty that English people enjoyed. By the 1820s Americans started to make extravagant claims about the extent and significance of their liberty. We can see it in a long poem (thirty-five stanzas) written by William Cullen Bryant in 1821. Although it is simply entitled "The Ages," the poem is meant to trace the evolution of human liberty through the ages. The ages are supposed to supply a historical backdrop and context for the leading figure, Liberty; but

47. Burke, "Speech on a Motion for Leave to Bring in a Bill to Repeal and Alter Certain Acts Respecting Religious Opinions" (May 11, 1792) in Bohn ed., *The Works of Edmund Burke,* 6:114; and see Dickinson, *Liberty and Property,* 287.

the featured attraction is kept in the wings for much of the poem — presumably because liberty has more often been an absence than a presence in human history. Since the poem begins with the very dawn of civilization — somewhere between the fall of man and the existence of human societies — liberty finally "awakens" in Greece at stanza 15 and doesn't make a significant comeback until stanza 33, when the colonists bring liberty to the New World, where presumably she lives happily ever after despite occasional vicissitudes.[48] Although the poem really does not have very much to say about liberty, its clear implication is that waiting several millennia to find a true home was worthwhile because the home turned out to be America. "The Ages" might be considered a poetic counterpart to George Bancroft's *History of the United States from the Discovery of America to the End of the Revolutionary War* — comparably epic, comparably cosmic, and incomparably dull.

Although we do not at first find large numbers of Americans who claimed distinctiveness for the character of liberty in the United States, virtually no one who discussed the subject acknowledged the existence of genuinely parallel developments or ideas elsewhere in the world. George McDuffie of South Carolina made a characteristically grandiose claim in the House of Representatives on February 15, 1826: "It is our propitious fortune to exist under a Government that has, in the main, answered all the great ends for which governments are instituted — enjoyed, in fact, a system of regulated liberty more perfect in its past operations than any which has hitherto existed in the world." Two years later Edward Everett echoed this belief that regulated liberty, if not invented in the United States, surely achieved its fullest flowering here.[49]

Everett also made a set of connections that most of his countrymen shared: between the growth of liberty, the efflorescence of prosperity, and the permanence that both of those cherished quali-

48. Parke Godwin, ed., *The Poetical Works of William Cullen Bryant* (New York, 1883), 1:53–67.

49. McDuffie is quoted in Charles Warren, *Congress, the Constitution, and the Supreme Court* (Boston, 1925), 2; Everett, "The History of Liberty," 152.

ties owed to written constitutions and legislative enactments. In that formulation he came a bit closer to describing a configuration that was, in several respects, distinctively American. In 1842, while serving as minister to Great Britain, Everett attended a dinner in Manchester and responded with this line to a toast given by the president of the British Association for the Promotion of Science: "Though we are ardently, passionately attached to liberty, it is liberty enshrined in constitutions, and organized by laws." On many other occasions, mostly back at home, Everett emphasized the special relationship between government, order, and prosperity in the United States. Speaking of the Philadelphia Convention of 1787, for example, he packed the whole formula into a single sentence: "In founding a strong and efficient government, adequate to the raising up of a powerful and prosperous people, their first step was to reject the institutions to which other governments traced their strength and prosperity, or had, at least, regarded as the necessary conditions of stability and order."[50]

Daniel Webster, more than any other prominent figure in nineteenth-century America, trumpeted the glories and special attributes of liberty in his native land. What Webster had to say about the glories was neither distinctive nor subtle: merely nationalistic. Speaking at Lexington, Massachusetts, in April 1835 at a commemorative ceremony, he praised the contribution of patriotic militiamen to the advancement of liberty, and ended on a familiar affirmative note: "The liberty and the Union of the United States, may both be perpetual."[51]

When he spoke about the American-ness of American liberty (and Webster often did) he sounded vague, chauvinistic, and not very thoughtful, though it is entirely possible that his words conveyed more meaning to contemporaries than they do to us. In 1833, for example, addressing the U.S. Senate in response to John C. Calhoun, Webster drew but did not explain or clarify a windy dis-

---

50. Everett, "British Association at Manchester," May 25, 1842, in Everett, *Orations and Speeches on Various Occasions,* 2:429; Everett, "The History of Liberty," 166.

51. *The Writings and Speeches of Daniel Webster* (Boston, 1903), 13:57–58.

tinction between political liberty (which we recall had been both good and American back in the 1770s and 80s) and "American liberty," whatever that meant. The context for this discussion, of course, was the Nullification Crisis pitting South Carolina against the national government. Even so, that situation sheds little light on Webster's usage, which was significant both because his speech was admired at the time and because schoolchildren would be required to memorize it for years to come. "The liberty which I think is staked on the contest," he said, "is not political liberty, in any general and undefined character, but our own well-understood and long-enjoyed *American* liberty." All that he added for our edification are the lines: "Guarded by constitutions and secured by union, it is that liberty which is our paternal inheritance. . . ."[52]

In a subsequent address Webster acknowledged that "liberty has existed in other times, in other countries, and in other forms," but it had been flawed in every instance. He admired several aspects of liberty in ancient Greece; "but still it was a liberty of disconnected states," unlike our own achievement of "Union and Liberty." He recognized a "proud, ambitious, domineering spirit" in Roman liberty; but condemned it on account of Rome's willingness to allow slavery in the outer provinces. American liberty, by contrast, "is characteristic, peculiar, and altogether our own. Nothing like it existed in former times. . . ." The roots of its distinctiveness, according to Webster, were republican institutions, above all "the establishment of popular governments, on the basis of representation," along with written constitutions "founded on the immediate authority of the people themselves, and regulating and restraining all the powers conferred upon government. . . ."[53]

For half a century thereafter, ceremonial events supplied occa-

52. Webster, "The Constitution not a Compact between Sovereign States," February 16, 1833, ibid., 6:183.

53. Webster, "The Addition to the Capitol," an address delivered in Washington, D.C., on July 4, 1851, ibid., 4:294, 297–98, 299–300. The criteria of written constitutions and unified states may explain the lack of interest by Webster's generation in Renaissance Venice, where liberty and order had also been prized. See William J. Bouwsma, *Venice*

sions for more of the same: public discourse in which liberty was invoked without clarification, claimed but not explained. When the Reverend Dr. Richard S. Storrs spoke on July 4, 1876, at the Academy of Music in New York, he chose the "Rise of Constitutional Liberty" as his subject. Although Storrs acknowledged that English liberty had been the parent of our own, Americans had expanded it. Their goal and ideal had been the achievement of private (read "individual") liberty combined with perfect public order. When Charles Francis Adams, Jr., spoke on the same day at Taunton, Massachusetts, an old community not far from Plymouth, he selected "The Progress of Liberty" as his topic. Adams included a formulaic and vague allusion to "the great law of liberty" that had been enunciated in 1776; and posed the rhetorical question: What had been most distinctive about the American during the first century since Independence? Adams's answer was equally predictable: "His devotion to the principle of liberty."[54]

Americans managed to persuade themselves that their political and social achievements were unique as well as highly successful. The nationalistic businessman-turned-historian, James Ford Rhodes, wrote to a friend in 1912 that "the manner in which we are working out our social problems in comparison with England, Germany, France and Italy seems to be more important than to measure the contribution of the Middle Ages to civilization. . . . I feel sure that we are coming out all right with neither the sacrifice of liberty nor order and with the results of civilization intact."[55] Throughout the nineteenth century many Americans were aware that Europeans, in particular, watched with interest to see whether

---

and the Defense of Republican Liberty: Renaissance Values in the Age of the Counter Reformation (Berkeley, 1968), II, 423–27.

54. The two speeches first appeared in *The New-York Tribune* and then, for wider and perhaps more permanent circulation, in an "Extra" pamphlet dated July 4, 1876. For Storrs, see 20, 23; for Adams, see 31, 36. See also an anonymous 39-page tract, *The History of Liberty* (Manlius, NY, 1874), esp. 21, 24–25.

55. Quoted in Robert Cruden, *James Ford Rhodes: The Man, the Historian, and His Work* (Cleveland, 1961), 139.

republican institutions and liberty constituted "a mockery, a pretence, and a curse,—or a blessing. . . ."[56]

No amount of evidence to the contrary could have persuaded them that the dynamics of American liberty were not distinctive. Jefferson had actually acquired from Lord Kames a convincing rationale for combining liberty with order; but no matter. Burke had written that the only liberty meaningful to him "is a liberty connected with order: and that not only exists with order and virtue, but which cannot exist at all without them." Over and over again, British political theorists and historians declared in print their gratitude for a heritage of constitutional freedom "reconciling liberty with order." Thomas Babington Macaulay and Goldwin Smith echoed Henry Hallam with variations on that theme. Walter Bagehot, the profoundly influential writer of mid-Victorian times, wanted to ascertain the conditions for reconciling freedom and progress with political stability. He found the answer in ordered liberty, as did William E. Gladstone in a widely noticed essay published in *The North American Review* in 1878.[57]

James Bryce, a sympathetic analyst of American political thought and institutions, noticed our naive provincialism in *The American Commonwealth* (1889). "Americans cherish the notion," he remarked, "that they are the only people who enjoy true political liberty, liberty far fuller than that of England, far more orderly than that of France."[58] Whether the American perception was no more than

---

56. Everett, The History of Liberty," 172.

57. For Jefferson and Kames see Ferguson, *Law and Letters in American Culture*, 57–58; for Burke see David Mathew, *Lord Acton and His Times* (University, AL, 1968), 82, 87, 162; for Hallam, Macaulay, and the Whig intellectuals, see J. W. Burrow, *A Liberal Descent: Victorian Historians and the English Past* (Cambridge, 1981), 39, 248, and Elisabeth Wallace, "Goldwin Smith on History," *Journal of Modern History* 26 (September 1954): 220; for Bagehot see Stefan Collini, Donald Winch, and John Burrow, *That Noble Science of Politics: A Study in Nineteenth-Century Intellectual History* (Cambridge, 1983), 164; Gladstone, "Kin Beyond Sea," *North American Review* 127 (September 1878): 179–212; and *New York Times*, May 30, 1901, p. 1.

58. Quoted in David M. Potter, *Freedom and Its Limitations in American Life* (Stanford, 1976), 2.

a delusion will remain forever a moot point. The disorder created by our Revolution may have been less severe than the disorder created by the French Revolution; but the disorders created by our Civil War surely must have been more bloody and prolonged than the ephemeral Revolution of 1848 in France.

Be that as it may, the point is moot because our concern here is culture and the realm of perception, values, and ideas. Writing in the later 1830s of his own society, Tocqueville believed that "my contemporaries fear disorder much more than servitude. . . . The world in our time is full of people who lightly value human dignity and who would willingly buy, with all the liberty of the human species, the right to sell their harvest in peace."[59] Toward the end of the century, Elie Halévy and his intellectual circle in France regarded the most vital problem of political organization as the maintenance of order, because without order liberty could not survive. The responsibility of government was to preserve both order and liberty so as to avoid tyranny on the one hand and anarchy on the other. Johan Huizinga made precisely the same point about political culture in The Netherlands during the nineteenth century.[60]

To muddle matters just a bit—though more for us, perhaps, than for those people we have under inquiry—it should be noted that many nineteenth-century Europeans conjured up images of liberty in America that coincided with and reinforced the American self-image.[61] Still other Europeans, meanwhile, saw the Americans as they wished to be seen but then proceeded to delineate strange or misleading contrasts with European attitudes toward liberty. Michel Chevalier, for example, visited the United States in 1833–35, published an account of his travels in 1836, and entitled one chapter

---

59. Quoted in James T. Schleifer, *The Making of Tocqueville's "Democracy in America"* (Chapel Hill, 1980), 180.

60. Myrna Chase, *Elie Halévy: An Intellectual Biography* (New York, 1980), 48–49; Huizinga, "The Spirit of the Netherlands" (1935) in Huizinga, *Dutch Civilisation in the Seventeenth Century and Other Essays* (New York, 1968), 128.

61. See Ray Allen Billington, *Land of Savagery, Land of Promise: The European Image of the American Frontier in the Nineteenth Century* (New York, 1981), 255–61.

"Authority and Liberty." It supplies a curious compound of penetrating and misleading observations. Two passages may suffice. American society, according to Chevalier, "is deeply imbued with the
sentiment of order. It has been nurtured in the hatred of the old
political systems of Europe, but a feeling of the need for self-restraint
runs through its veins. It is divided between . . . its thirst after freedom and its hunger for social order." That much is unexception-
able; but the comparison drawn by Chevalier later in the same
chapter is a peculiar blend of perception and distortion:

> For us, the French, who resemble each other in nothing except in differing
> from everybody else, for us, to whom variety is as necessary as the air, to
> whom a life of rules would be a subject of horror, the Yankee system would
> be torture. Their liberty is not the liberty to outrage all that is sacred on
> earth, to set religion at defiance, to laugh morals to scorn, to undermine the
> foundations of social order, to mock at all traditions and all received opin-
> ions; it is neither the liberty of being a monarchist in a republican country,
> nor that of sacrificing the honor of the poor man's wife or daughter to one's
> base passions; it is not even the liberty to enjoy one's wealth by a public
> display, for public opinion has its sumptuary laws to which all must conform
> under pain of moral outlawry; nor even that of living in private differently
> from the rest of the world. The liberty of the Yankee is essentially limited
> and special like the nature of the race.[62]

During the middle and later nineteenth century, observers of the
American scene, and especially British writers, became alarmed by
the implications that "excessive" democracy and mass culture seemed
to portend for liberty, both at home and in the United States. Macaulay, whose letters to Henry S. Randall in 1857 were published,
expressed the fear that purely democratic institutions posed a grave
threat to liberty; but because he valued civilization above all, he
would not object to the sacrifice of liberty in order to save civilization. William Edward Hartpole Lecky, who was almost a generation younger than Macaulay—a late Victorian, as it were—
elaborated upon Macaulay's views in *Democracy and Liberty* (1896),

---

62. Chevalier, *Society, Manners, and Politics in the United States: Letters on North America*, edited by John William Ward (Ithaca, 1961), 321, 327–28.

which was widely read and came to be regarded as a classic. Democracy, in Lecky's opinion, was not necessarily favorable to liberty; and equality, he believed, was naturally dangerous to liberty: "Democracy destroys the balance of opinions, interests, and classes, on which constitutional liberty mainly depends." Democracy, he concluded, "may often prove the direct opposite of liberty."[63]

The Anglo-American elite shared that pessimistic outlook. The middle class in the United States might have been perplexed by it. But American society in the central decades of the nineteenth century was even more perplexed by the greatest crisis of liberty, property, and authority in its entire history.

So much has already been written about the Nullification Crisis of 1829–33, about the problem of slavery in American culture, and about the sectional disputes of the midnineteenth century that we can (and must) proceed selectively in integrating them here. It would be inappropriate if not impossible, however, to discuss the concept of liberty in nineteenth-century thought without indicating the role played by those three major issues and their impact upon the meaning of liberty in America.

For John C. Calhoun, more than a quarter of a century devoted to the defense of sectional interests and state sovereignty prompted an extended series of treatises upon various aspects of liberty. Few of Calhoun's comments are unexpected by now, and the most systematic were not published until after his death in 1850. They are important, nonetheless, because of their influence upon southern leaders throughout the sectional crisis and because of their originality. Calhoun's political thought could be perverse (by our lights); but it is also notable for rigorous logic and the analytical power of his exposition. His points of departure sound familiar. He re-

63. Richard C. Beatty, *Lord Macaulay: Victorian Liberal* (Norman, OK, 1938), 365–66; Lecky, *Democracy and Liberty*, edited by William Murchison (Indianapolis, 1981), 1:217–19.

membered his father having "maintained that government to be best which allowed the largest amount of individual liberty compatible with social order and tranquility." Understandably, when Calhoun wrote of "liberty and security" in *A Disquisition on Government*, he really meant liberty and order. Liberty must always yield to "protection" (i.e., order), and liberty should not be extended to the point where it might weaken government.[64]

Although Calhoun recognized the need for both power and liberty, and addressed himself in several ways to the relationship between liberty and authority, his criteria for delineating the boundaries between them were not very precise. He liked to say that by assigning each one, liberty and authority, to its appropriate sphere, all conflicts between them could be resolved. Attractive as the notion of liberty's very own sphere may be, however, Calhoun found it difficult to delineate that sphere in a way that could be practically applied by those who had to wrestle with the nastiest public issues of the nineteenth century.[65]

Nevertheless, Calhoun's most noteworthy contribution lay in his explanation of why his theory of the concurrent majority was more advantageous for liberty. Here is the core of his argument:

> The more perfectly a government combines power and liberty—that is, the greater its power and the more enlarged and secure the liberty of individuals —the more perfectly it fulfills the ends for which government is ordained. To show, then, that the government of the concurrent majority is better calculated to fulfill them than that of the numerical, it is only necessary to explain why the former is better suited to combine a higher degree of power and a wider scope of liberty than the latter. . . . The concurrent majority, then, is better suited to enlarge and secure the bounds of liberty because it is better suited to prevent government from passing beyond its proper limits and to restrict it to its primary end—the protection of the community. But in doing this, it leaves necessarily all beyond it open and free to individual exertions, and thus enlarges and secures the sphere of liberty to the greatest

64. August O. Spain, *The Political Theory of John C. Calhoun* (New York, 1968), 35; Calhoun, *A Disquisition on Government and Selections from the Discourse*, edited by C. Gordon Post (New York, 1953), 40, 42.

65. Spain, *Political Theory of Calhoun*, 101, 105.

extent which the condition of the community will admit. . . . The tendency of government to pass beyond its proper limits is what exposes liberty to danger and renders it insecure; and it is the strong counteraction of governments of the concurrent majority to this tendency which makes them so favorable to liberty.[66]

Calhoun's ruminations on liberty and equality, a topic that concerned him on several occasions, do not make pleasant reading because we know all too well the racial prejudices that underpinned them. Large numbers of contemporaries shared his attitude, however, and it forms a major link in the chain of American ideas about liberty during the nineteenth century. In a speech given to the Senate in 1848, Calhoun explained that "the quantum of power on the part of the government, and of liberty on that of individuals, instead of being equal in all cases, must necessarily be very unequal among different people, according to their different conditions." The more ignorant, debased, and corrupt people are, the more power government must have in order to preserve society against anarchy. Under such circumstances, a diminution of individual liberty is justified. As members of society rise on the ladders of intelligence, virtue, and patriotism, the need for governmental power lessens and the proportion of individual liberty increases.[67]

In his *Disquisition*, which Calhoun was working on at the time of this speech, he phrased even more bluntly the assumption that large numbers of northerners as well as southerners presumed to be valid: "It is a great and dangerous error to suppose that all peo-

66. Calhoun, *A Disquisition on Government*, 45–46. Although historians of American culture and political thought have not previously suggested any connection, I am persuaded that Francis Lieber's counterbalanced formulation of civil liberty as the dual necessity for both power and liberty, written during the Civil War, developed in response to Calhoun's ideas. (Lieber taught history and political economy at the College of South Carolina from 1835 until 1856.) Lieber insisted that the very essence of civil liberty required a system of checks to control the will of the supreme power. See Bernard E. Brown, *American Conservatives: The Political Thought of Francis Lieber and John W. Burgess* (New York, 1951), 61, 72–73.

67. "Speech on the Oregon Bill," June 27, 1848, in Richard K. Crallé, ed., *The Works of John C. Calhoun* (Charleston, 1851), 4:510–11.

ple are equally entitled to liberty. It is a reward to be earned, not a blessing to be gratuitously lavished on all alike. . . . Every effort to disturb or defeat [this pattern], by attempting to elevate a people in the scale of liberty above the point to which they are entitled to rise, must ever prove abortive. . . ."[68]

Calhoun, as we well know, provoked hostile responses. At the time of the Nullification Crisis, John Quincy Adams replied in terms entirely consistent with the balance most strongly valued and sought in nineteenth-century America. Nullification is the provocation, he declared, "to that brutal and foul contest of force, which has hitherto baffled all the efforts of the European, and Southern American nations, to introduce among them constitutional governments of liberty and order."[69]

Calhoun's impassioned defense of chattel slavery as a positive good only intensified a debate over slavery that had been pricking the nation's conscience ever since the late eighteenth century. During the mid-1790s a French visitor remarked that "the American people, so excited about their own liberty, don't consider the liberty of others unless it suits their political convenience." It is indeed true that the familiar slogan "liberty and property" acquired special meaning in the antebellum South as a rationale for the protection and preservation of the peculiar institution. Alexander H. Stephens of Georgia, who became Vice President of the Confederacy, would cite the U.S. Constitution in order to bolster his section's contention that no person (meaning no adult white male, of course) could be deprived of life, liberty, or property without due process of law.[70]

68. Calhoun, *A Disquisition on Government*, 43–44.

69. Adams, *An Oration Addressed to the Citizens of the Town of Quincy, on the Fourth of July, 1831* . . . (Boston, 1831), 36. See also the statement, made in Ohio in 1832, that Nullification was unacceptable because it was "calculated to overthrow the great temple of American liberty." Quoted in John Bach MacMaster, "A Century of Constitutional Interpretation," *The Century Magazine* 37 (April 1889): 873.

70. Kenneth and Anna M. Roberts, eds., *Moreau de St. Méry's American Journey* [1793–1798] (Garden City, NY, 1947), 310; George Fitzhugh and Stephens are cited in Edmund Wilson, *Patriotic Gore: Studies in the Literature of the American Civil War* (New

In the North, however, a gradual reconsideration occurred, one that did not disregard the legal obligations of property, but made the moral compunctions of liberty more prominent. The state of New Jersey, for example, adopted gradual abolition in 1804. Masters did not have a strong basis for claiming that their property was being confiscated, because their slaves were not set free directly. Rather, masters simply lost the right to have the services for life of their slaves' children. Property rights of masters were further protected by requiring that children emancipated under the 1804 law spend many years working for the masters who owned their mothers — a form of compensation for the expense of raising those black children until they became old enough to work and be productive. New York had adopted a similar provision five years earlier, but repealed it because of the vast expense entailed, combined with suspicions of widespread fraud.[71]

Despite the hesitant and sometimes hypocritical "progress" that took place between the later 1790s and the 1830s, changes began to occur once the nation's consciousness was raised and its conscience aroused. In 1825 the U.S. Supreme Court had to respond to the awkward case created by a notorious vessel named *The Antelope*, a case concerning the legality of the slave trade under international law. An American man-of-war captured a ship carrying nearly three hundred Africans to be sold as slaves. Because these Africans had previously been taken from Portuguese and Spanish slave ships, authorities in those countries petitioned the Supreme Court to direct the return of their lawful property. John Marshall's agonized decision acknowledged that this complex case had brought the "sacred rights of liberty and property" into conflict. He reluc-

York, 1962), 351, 393. See also Albert Taylor Bledsoe, *An Essay on Liberty and Slavery* (Philadelphia, 1856); and Brown, *Origin and Growth of Civil Liberty in Maryland*, 19. Brown emphasized the need for control, "regulated freedom," and the fear of licentiousness and anarchy.

71. Arthur Zilversmit, "Liberty and Property: New Jersey and the Abolition of Slavery," *New Jersey History* 88 (Winter 1970): 223. Cf. Robert M. Cover, *Justice Accused: Antislavery and the Judicial Process* (New Haven, 1975), 67.

tantly concluded that "this Court must not yield to feelings which might seduce it from the path of duty, but must obey the mandates of the law."[72]

An active campaign to elevate moral considerations above legal technicalities became sufficiently aggressive by the later 1830s so that it could no longer be ignored. In 1837 an antislavery group published a 227-page compilation of readings, simply entitled *Liberty*, designed to show that slavery violated both civil and natural law. In 1838 Theodore Dwight Weld took the customary motto "liberty and property" and turned it around by arguing that the perpetuation of slavery deprived Negroes of their liberty and property without due process of law.[73]

During the 1840s, moreover, several of the leading Transcendentalists added their voices to this chorus, offering the argument that under current conditions a fundamental conflict existed between liberty and property and then resolving the conflict by introducing the idea of a "higher law" that justified the supremacy of liberty. Such Transcendentalists as Theodore Parker urged a personal as well as a societal repudiation of evil, which primarily meant the rejection of slavery even though some Americans insisted that slaves were an especially "sacred" form of property. Moral law became a weapon mobilized on behalf of human rights and in opposition to traditional notions of property rights.[74]

By 1847 advocates of antislavery in New York began to use the phrase "liberty and humanity" as an antidote to proslavery arguments and a rebuke to northern jurists who insisted that the Fugi-

72. John T. Noonan, *The Antelope: The Ordeal of the Recaptured Africans in the Administrations of James Monroe and John Quincy Adams* (Berkeley, 1977), 43, 45–46, 59–60, 62–64, 101, 104, 112, 115, 123, 128, 140, 150–52; Leon Friedman and Fred L. Israel, eds., *The Justices of the United States Supreme Court, 1789–1978: Their Lives and Major Opinions* (New York, 1980), 1:518–19; Francis N. Stites, *John Marshall: Defender of the Constitution* (Boston, 1981), 148.

73. William M. Wiecek, *The Sources of Antislavery Constitutionalism in America, 1760–1848* (Ithaca, 1977), 190, 209, 287.

74. Parker, *The Function and Place of Conscience in Relation to the Laws of Men: A Sermon for the Times, Preached at the Melodeon . . . Sept. 22, 1850* (Boston, 1850).

tive Slave Law would have to be enforced. A sermon preached in 1856 by Noah Porter, the President of Yale College, redefined civil liberty in order to contend "that where the spirit of Slavery is, there is not liberty." Slavery infringed upon civil liberty, he argued, because it defied the concept that all men are created equal, upon which the nation had been established. According to Porter, civil liberty "implies firm guarantees of personal liberty" because under our system of government a threefold principle was operative: that every man's home is his castle, that general warrants are unconstitutional, and that the Habeas Corpus Act must be observed.[75]

Owing to the bitterness of the dispute over slavery—the institution's existence as well as its expansion into the territories—Americans of divergent persuasions felt compelled to act upon conscience, to respond to a higher law by flouting "mere" statutes, or to defend their liberty and property—by violence if necessary. The growth of mob action and the fear of anarchy resulted in an augmentation of the rhetoric of ordered liberty. We find it among such southerners as Governor Henry A. Wise of Virginia, George Fitzhugh of Virginia, and Alexander H. Stephens of Georgia.[76]

We also find it in the fiction of James Fenimore Cooper at midcentury, and in the pronouncements of the "doughface" presidents throughout the 1850s. Franklin Pierce's second annual message to Congress, late in 1854, was typical: "We have to maintain inviolate the great doctrine of the inherent right of popular self-government; to reconcile the largest liberty of the individual citizen with complete security of the public order."[77]

For various reasons about which much has already been written —including anticonscription riots in the North, an excess of states'

75. See Thomas D. Morris, *Free Men All: The Personal Liberty Laws of the North, 1780–1861* (Baltimore, 1974), 122; Noah Porter, *Civil Liberty: A Sermon Preached in Farmington, Connecticut, July 13, 1856* (New York, 1856), esp. 6, 18, 20.

76. Bernard Mayo, *Myths and Men: Patrick Henry, George Washington, Thomas Jefferson* (Athens, GA, 1959), 25; Wilson, *Patriotic Gore*, 358, 362, 410.

77. Jones, *Pursuit of Happiness*, 111–12; Richardson, ed., *Messages and Papers of the Presidents*, 5:292. For other examples of the anxiety caused by disorder appearing to verge upon anarchy, see Lincoln's famous "Address Before the Young Men's Lyceum of Spring-

rights in the South, and secession itself—the Civil War prompted large numbers of Americans to reconsider the ideal of achieving a *balance* between liberty and order in favor of *subordinating* the former to the latter. In 1863, for example, Charles J. Stillé, an influential lawyer and historian in Philadelphia, delivered a speech entitled "The Historical Development of American Civilization." He insisted that the founders of the nation had been law-abiding Englishmen, that the American system of government was not revolutionary, that liberty without order was unthinkable, and that restraints must be placed upon liberty, especially individual liberty, in order to fulfill the needs of the community more adequately.[78]

That position was by no means universally shared throughout the North. Those who felt concerned about Lincoln's handling of the press and habeas corpus were prompted to speak out on behalf of "our own American institutions . . . liberty of speech, liberty of the press, liberty of the person." But despite numerous expressions of concern along those lines, the war provided a major impetus toward a conservative view of liberty that emphasized order, community, and a Burkean sense of national continuity. By 1865 such diverse northerners as Horace Bushnell, Herman Melville, and Henry W. Bellows contended vigorously that the foremost social need was the maintenance of order, an objective best achieved by the combined forces of law and religion.[79]

During the post-war years these feelings intensified, with the re-

---

field, Illinois," January 27, 1838, in Roy P. Basler, ed., *The Collected Works of Abraham Lincoln* (New Brunswick, NJ, 1953), 1:109–11; and Porter, *Civil Liberty: A Sermon Preached in Farmington, 5.*

78. See Joseph Tuthill Duryea, *Civil Liberty. A Sermon Preached on the National Thanksgiving Day, August 6, 1863* (New York, 1863), 6, 8, 14, 16, 18, 21; Phillip S. Paludan, "The American Civil War Considered as a Crisis in Law and Order," *American Historical Review* 77 (October 1972): 1017, 1033–34; for Stillé see George M. Fredrickson, *The Inner Civil War: Northern Intellectuals and the Crisis of the Union* (New York, 1965), 141–43.

79. See Edward Ingersoll, *Personal Liberty and Martial Law: A Review of Some Pamphlets of the Day* (Philadelphia, 1862), 3; Fredrickson, *The Inner Civil War,* 185. According to legend, the "novel" American bank robbery took place in Liberty, Missouri, early in 1866. See Richard M. Dorson, *American Folklore* (Chicago, 1959), 239.

sult that liberty, when discussed at all, was linked to the need for strengthened government, "sound planning," and the "organizing power of liberty." The most influential expounder of American law and constitutionalism during the final third of the nineteenth century, Judge Thomas M. Cooley, preached a gospel of liberty and order. Party platforms were most likely to favor "the largest individual liberty consistent with public order"; and during the 1880s essayists emphasized that the Anglo-Saxon peoples had demonstrated, above all others, how to combine liberty with order.[80]

Two pertinent trends appeared during the later 1880s and 90s. The first is neither unexpected nor particularly complicated. Given the emergence by 1884 of what Wendell Phillips called "the labor question," given the controversies that arose over the right of labor to strike, given the rise of intense class consciousness and conflict, it seems in retrospect altogether predictable that tradition-oriented Americans would feel apprehensive about social disorder, real and imagined. Law and Order leagues sprang up hither and yon between 1885 and 1887. The first one appeared in Sedalia, Missouri; but they spread swiftly from Kansas City to Richmond. Organized to protect businesses from labor boycotts, they tended to be semi-secret in nature, as well as pro-property, and their members socially respectable.[81] Unlike William Graham Sumner, a conservative social theorist who regarded strikes and social disorder as inevitable

---

80. See Andrew Dickson White, *The Most Bitter Foe of Nations, and the Way to Its Permanent Overthrow* (New Haven, 1866), 34; Morton Keller, *Affairs of State: Public Life in Late Nineteenth Century America* (Cambridge, MA, 1977), 43, 554; John F. Aiken, *The History of Liberty* (New York, 1877); Wallace D. Farnham, "The Weakened Spring of Government: A Study in Nineteenth-Century American History," *American Historical Review* 68 (April 1963): 662–80; Paludan, *A Covenant with Death*, 259; Cruden, *James Ford Rhodes*, 32.

81. Phillips, *The Labor Question* (Boston, 1884), 5, 6; Leon Fink, *Workingmen's Democracy: The Knights of Labor and American Politics* (Urbana, 1983), 122, 127, 130, 139, 163, 167, 175.

by-products of liberty ("Industrial war is, in fact, an incident of liberty," 1889), members of the Law and Order leagues did not.[82]

On the occasion of the Constitution's Centennial in 1887, no theme was heard with greater frequency than the imperative that liberty must be modulated by order. Much of the praise lavished upon the Constitution insisted that it provided the foundation and guidelines for liberty with order. The Episcopal Bishop of Atlanta expressed a characteristic sentiment of the day: namely, that the Constitution was truly "the 'Magna Carta' of American liberty, which is just as far removed from license, as Law is from disorder."[83]

The second trend to appear at that time was considerably more significant and complicated. It has been written about and placed in historical context by Edward S. Corwin in a brief but classic analysis called *Liberty Against Government* (1948). Despite the apparent connotation of that title, however, the real issue at stake was not one of liberty and order but rather one of liberty and property. In essence, between about 1884 and 1934 the U.S. Supreme Court broadened the concept of property, broadened the concept of liberty in such a way that "property" could be folded into it, and then applied what amounted to extraconstitutional guarantees to both.

Prior to 1866, when Congress passed the Fourteenth Amendment, the concept of liberty had not figured very prominently in American constitutional theory. Over the subsequent seventeen years, however, a phrase found in Section One of that amendment —"nor shall any state deprive any person of life, liberty, or property, without due process of law"—resulted in "liberty" becoming a judicially construable term, primarily understood as freedom of

82. Sumner is quoted in Keller, *Affairs of State*, 395. See also Frank Tariello, Jr., *The Reconstruction of American Political Ideology, 1865–1917* (Charlottesville, 1982), 43, 155.

83. See Thomas A. Becker to John Kasson, et al., September 6, 1887, Constitution Centennial Commission Papers, box 1, Historical Society of Pennsylvania, Philadelphia; Kilian O. Flasch to Kasson, August 20, 1887, ibid.; A. Cleveland Coxe to Kasson, September 3, 1887, ibid.; a Resolution passed by the Bunker Hill Monument Association, June 17, 1887, and sent to the Centennial Commission in Philadelphia, ibid., box 3.

contract (often expressed as freedom to contract, i.e., to make a contractual arrangement). Under the auspices of laissez faire economic thought, the traditional meaning of liberty as physical freedom and governmental protection of personal rights was expanded to include such questions as how long a person might work in a given day. When that happened, in the controversial 5-to-4 decision known as *Lochner v. New York* (1905), Justice Oliver Wendell Holmes, dissenting, declared that the majority had "perverted" the proper meaning of the word "liberty" in the Fourteenth Amendment.[84] History eventually vindicated Holmes and repudiated that majority of five, but not until the 1930s, a full generation later.

Initially it looked as though History would vindicate Justice Stephen J. Field, who wrote influential dissenting opinions in two of the most important cases to emerge after the Civil War. In the first, known collectively as the *Slaughter-House Cases* (1873), a majority of the justices upheld the right of Louisiana's state legislature to grant a monopoly for slaughtering livestock in the New Orleans area to a single corporation. The various and sundry butchers who were unable to work on their own premises as a result of this monopoly brought suit and lost. But Justices Field, Bradley, and Swayne wrote strident dissents that struck a common note and set the tone for more than half a century to come.[85]

- *Justice Field, invoking the Fourteenth Amendment:*
All monopolies in any known trade or manufacture are an invasion of these privileges, for they encroach upon the liberty of citizens to acquire property and pursue happiness. . . .

84. See Corwin, *The Twilight of the Supreme Court: A History of Our Constitutional Theory* (New Haven, 1934), 78–80; Corwin, *Court Over Constitution: A Study of Judicial Review as an Instrument of Popular Government* (Princeton, 1938), 108–9; and for the wording of Holmes's dissent, see Stanley I. Kutler, ed., *The Supreme Court and the Constitution: Readings in American Constitutional History* (2nd ed.: New York, 1977), 288–89.

85. All of the opinions in the *Slaughter-House Cases*, including Justice Miller's for the Court, will be found at 16 Wallace 36. Field's covers 83–111, the quotation at 101. Bradley's covers 111–24, the quotations at 115–16 and 122. Swayne's covers 124–30, the quotation at 127.

- *Justice Bradley, insisting that ever since Magna Carta, life, liberty, and property had been deemed inviolable except by due process of law:*
This right to choose one's calling is an essential part of that liberty which it is the right of government to protect; and a calling, when chosen, is a man's property and right. Liberty and property are not protected when these rights are arbitrarily assailed. . . . A law which prohibits a large class of citizens from adopting a lawful employment previously adopted, does deprive them of liberty as well as property, without due process of law. Their right of choice is a portion of their liberty; their occupation is their property.
- *Justice Swayne:*
Liberty is freedom from all restraints but such as are justly imposed by law. Beyond that line lies the domain of usurpation and tyranny."

Justice Field dissented once again in *Munn v. Illinois* (1877), a highly controversial case in which the Court upheld the Illinois state legislature's right to regulate rates charged by the owners of grain elevators. In seeking to protect private property from intervention by the state, Field explained that this business enterprise really was not "clothed" with a public interest. Why? Because the owner had not declared it to be. Nothing in the character of the warehousing business, Field insisted, justified governmental interference. Rather, by the term "liberty" in the Fourteenth Amendment "something more is meant than mere freedom from physical restraint or the bounds of a prison. It means freedom to go where one may choose, and to act in such manner, not inconsistent with the equal rights of others, as his judgment may dictate for the promotion of his happiness; that is, to pursue such callings and avocations as may be most suitable to develop his capacities, and give to them their highest enjoyment."[86]

In 1884 the Court effectively reversed its decision in the *Slaughter-House Cases*. In that same year Justice Field asserted that the Four-

---

86. *Munn v. Illinois*, 94 U.S. 113 (1877), the quotation at 142. Chief Justice Morrison R. Waite wrote the opinion of the Court, at 123-36. See also Howard Jay Graham, *Everyman's Constitution: Historical Essays on the Fourteenth Amendment, the "Conspiracy Theory," and American Constitutionalism* (Madison, 1968); and for a revisionist view, Michael Les Benedict, "Laissez-Faire and Liberty: A Re-evaluation of the Meaning and Origins of Laissez-Faire Constitutionalism," *Law and History Review* 3 (Fall 1985): 293-331.

teenth Amendment protected the title to a person's property as well as his liberty to control its use and enjoy its income – a novel proposition in American constitutional law that would have a profound effect upon the interaction of government and economic activity for almost half a century. The apotheosis of laissez faire had been achieved, and the writings of its prophets now appeared in profusion.[87]

Liberty and property became the dominant slogan for a distinctive era in the history of American enterprise; and a series of landmark decisions led the way for those best situated to benefit from them. The case of *Allgeyer v. Louisiana* (1897) affirmed the liberty of individuals to enter into contracts, however disadvantageous, without state regulation or interference. The case of *Coppage v. Kansas* (1915) extended freedom of contract to so-called "yellow-dog" contracts (ones in which as a condition of employment the worker agrees not to remain in or to join a union).[88] One extract from Justice Pitney's opinion for the Court demonstrates how the language of liberty could be manipulated in such a way that freedom for workers might be circumscribed in reality:

> If Congress is prevented from arbitrary interference with the liberty of contract because of the "due process" provisions of the Fifth Amendment, it is too clear for argument that the States are prevented from the like interference by virtue of the corresponding clause of the Fourteenth Amendment; and hence if it be unconstitutional for Congress to deprive an employer

87. See Charles W. McCurdy, "Justice Field and the Jurisprudence of Government-Business Relations: Some Parameters of Laissez-Faire Constitutionalism, 1863–1897," *Journal of American History* 61 (March 1975): 973, 1005; Benjamin R. Twiss, *Lawyers and the Constitution: How Laissez Faire Came to the Supreme Court* (Princeton, 1942), 27–29, 50–52, 83, 89, 106–7, 154; Jones, *The Pursuit of Happiness*, 39–41; and John W. Burgess, *The Reconciliation of Government with Liberty* (New York, 1915), 299, 308, 358. For the compatibility between laissez faire and liberty and order, see Carl L. Becker, *Freedom and Responsibility in the American Way of Life* (1945: reprint, New York, 1958), 101.

88. *Allgeyer v. Louisiana*, 165 U.S. 578 (1897); *Coppage v. Kansas*, 236 U.S. 1 (1915). Key extracts from both opinions are reprinted in James Morton Smith and Paul L. Murphy, eds., *Liberty and Justice: A Historical Record of American Constitutional Development* (New York, 1958), 337–40.

of liberty or property for threatening an employee with loss of employment or discriminating against him because of his membership in a labor organization, it is unconstitutional for a State to similarly punish an employer for requiring his employee, as a condition of securing or retaining employment, to agree not to become or remain a member of such an organization while so employed. . . .

Included in the right of personal liberty and the right of private property — partaking of the nature of each — is the right to make contracts for the acquisition of property. Chief among such contracts is that of personal employment, by which labor and other services are exchanged for money or other forms of property. If this right be struck down or arbitrarily interfered with, there is a substantial impairment of liberty in the long-established constitutional sense. The right is as essential to the laborer as to the capitalist, to the poor as to the rich; for the vast majority of persons have no other honest way to begin to acquire property, save by working for money.[89]

The nadir in this sustained revisionism and attack upon the right of state government to act in a regulative capacity for the public interest occurred in *Adkins v. Children's Hospital* (1923), when the Court declared unconstitutional a minimum wage law for women. Once again the Court's opinion, written this time by Justice Sutherland, seems to combine a Darwinian faith as relentless as Calvinism with candor so lacking in guile that we feel centuries rather than decades must lie between us and this *ancien régime.*

> The statute now under consideration is attacked upon the ground that it authorizes an unconstitutional interference with the freedom of contract included within the guaranties of the due process clause of the Fifth Amendment. That the right to contract about one's affairs is a part of the liberty of the individual protected by this clause is settled by the decisions of this Court and is no longer open to question. . . . Within this liberty are contracts of employment of labor. In making such contracts, generally speaking, the parties have an equal right to obtain from each other the best terms they can as the result of private bargaining. . . .
>
> There is, of course, no such thing as absolute freedom of contract. It is subject to a great variety of restraints. But freedom of contract is, nevertheless, the general rule and restraint the exception; and the exercise of legisla-

89. *Coppage v. Kansas,* 236 U.S. 1 (1915), the quotations at 11 and 14.

tive authority to abridge it can be justified only by the existence of exceptional circumstances. . . .

It has been said that legislation of the kind now under review is required in the interest of social justice, for whose ends freedom of contract may lawfully be subjected to restraint. The liberty of the individual to do as he pleases, even in innocent matters, is not absolute. It must frequently yield to the common good, and the line beyond which the power of interference may not be pressed is neither definite nor unalterable but may be made to move, within limits not well defined, with changing need and circumstance. Any attempt to fix a rigid boundary would be unwise and futile.[90]

Justice Holmes dissented once again, and made no effort to conceal his contempt for the majority opinion and for a general trend that he had observed uncomfortably during his twenty years on the Court. Earlier decisions that applied the Fifth and Fourteenth amendments to relations between capital and labor at least "went no farther than an unpretentious assertion of the liberty to follow the ordinary callings," Holmes wrote. "Later that innocuous generality was expanded into the dogma, Liberty of Contract. Contract is not specially mentioned in the text that we have to construe [the due process clause]. It is merely an example of doing what you want to do, embodied in the word liberty."[91]

Holmes's disdain fell on deaf ears, however, and a reorientation did not begin to occur for more than a decade. The case of *Nebbia v. New York* (1934), decided two years after Holmes's retirement, marked the end of an era because it initiated a process whereby the relationship between liberty and property would be redefined in favor of the public interest as interpreted by the state. Justice Roberts presented the Court's opinion in *Nebbia*, a case involving minimum and maximum prices for milk: "The court has repeatedly sustained curtailment of enjoyment of private property, in the public interest. The owner's right may be subordinated to the needs

90. *Adkins v. Children's Hospital*, 261 U.S. 525 (1923). The essence of Sutherland's opinion is reprinted in Smith and Murphy, eds., *Liberty and Justice*, 382–83.

91. *Adkins v. Children's Hospital*, 261 U.S. 525 (1923), the quotation at 568. See also Holmes's earlier dissent in *Adair v. U.S.*, 208 U.S. 161 (1908), at 190; and Roscoe Pound, "Liberty of Contract," *Yale Law Journal* 18 (May 1909): 454–87, esp. 455.

of other private owners whose pursuits are vital to the paramount interests of the community." Back in 1885, in the case of *Barbier v. Connolly,* the U.S. Supreme Court had declared that the Fourteenth Amendment does not impair the police power of a state.[92] Almost half a century later, completing a 180-degree turnabout, the Court returned to a modified version of its 1885 stance.

One unfinished piece of pertinent business remained — the reversal of *Adkins v. Children's Hospital.* It occurred in 1937 — a year of dramatic transition in so many respects — in the case of *West Coast Hotel Co. v. Parrish.* At issue was the constitutional validity of a minimum wage law passed by the State of Washington. Chief Justice Charles Evans Hughes acknowledged that deprivation of liberty to contract without due process of law is forbidden by the Constitution; but he added, in the spirit of *Nebbia,* that "restraint or regulation of this liberty, if reasonable in relation to its subject and if adopted for the protection of the community against evils menacing the health, safety, morals and welfare of the people, is due process." The Court had at last explicitly redefined that strange sophistry called "substantive due process" begotten by the age of laissez faire. "What is this freedom?" Hughes asked.

> The Constitution does not speak of freedom of contract. It speaks of liberty and prohibits the deprivation of liberty without due process of law. In prohibiting that deprivation the Constitution does not recognize an absolute and uncontrollable liberty. Liberty in each of its phases has its history and connotation. But the liberty safeguarded is liberty in a social organization which requires the protection of law against the evils which menace the health, safety, morals and welfare of the people. Liberty under the Constitution is thus necessarily subject to the restraints of due process, and regulation which is reasonable in relation to its subject and is adopted in the interests of the community is due process.[93]

How tidy it would be if we could conclude this section by saying that an intellectual somersault had re-legitimized the older

92. *Nebbia v. New York,* 291 U.S. 502 (1934), the quotation at 525; *Barbier v. Connolly,* 113 U.S. 27 (1885), esp. at 31.

93. *West Coast Hotel Co. v. Parrish, et al.,* 300 U.S. 379 (1937), the quotation at 391. See also the decision in *National Labor Relations Board v. Jones & Laughlin Steel Corpora-*

nineteenth-century notion of "regulated liberty." Isn't that what Hughes seems to be saying? Yes and no. When jurists and journalists used the phrase "regulated liberty" during the middle third of the nineteenth century, they referred to self-control, the voluntary abdication of antisocial behavior with as little pressure from governmental institutions as possible.[94] When the Court implied or spoke of regulated liberty during the 1930s, however, it acknowledged that socio-economic complexities which could not have been imagined half a century earlier justified or even required an activist role for governmental institutions.

In 1941 Edward S. Corwin summarized the new wisdom: "Then as to the 'due process' clause, the word 'property' therein does not forbid the use by government of public funds for the *immediate* benefit of private persons in the realization of an *ulterior* public end; while the term 'liberty' in the clause includes 'fundamental rights,' like that of labor to organize and bargain collectively, which can often be more effectively asserted by means of legislation than by judicial review. The clause is, therefore, broad enough to lend positive constitutional sanction to projects of social reform—it is not solely a constitutional barrier."[95]

---

tion, 301 U.S. 1 (1937), from which a lengthy extract appears in Kutler, ed., *The Supreme Court and the Constitution*, 394–401. It is misleading to assume, however, that no breakthroughs or anticipations of change occurred prior to *Nebbia* in 1934. The Court often renders decisions that appear aberrant in the longer context of a historical continuum. In 1911, for example, Charles Evans Hughes wrote the Court's opinion in *Chicago, Burlington and Quincy Railroad Company v. McGuire*, 219 U.S. 549. "Freedom of contract is a qualified and not an absolute right. There is no absolute freedom to do as one wills or to contract as one chooses. The guaranty of liberty does not withdraw from legislative supervision that wide department of activity which consists of the making of contracts, or deny to government the power to provide restrictive safeguards. Liberty implies the absence of arbitrary restraint, not immunity from reasonable regulations and prohibitions imposed in the interests of the community." The Court upheld the claim of a brakeman who had been injured through negligence by the railroad. The brakeman based his claim upon Iowa state law, but the state's supreme court had ruled against him. The U.S. Supreme Court overruled the state court. The quotation at 567.

94. See the opinions quoted in Jones, *The Pursuit of Happiness*, 38 (1855), and Warren, *Supreme Court in United States History*, 3:184–85 (1867).

95. Corwin, *Constitutional Revolution, Ltd.* (Claremont, CA, 1941), 79. See also Mark

If the reassessment of those two consequential legal concepts, liberty and property and liberty of contract, did not achieve completion until 1937, it becomes more comprehensible that liberty and order also lingered on, as a commonplace in our political vocabulary, as well. The period of reformist activism that we call the Progressive Era encompassed a great deal of diversity. Although new views of liberty did start to surface early in the century, a majority of Americans did not yet subscribe to them. In this respect, also, fulfillment of a dream did not occur until Franklin D. Roosevelt's second term. The dream had to be articulated, however, so that a new generation could be nourished on it, and J. Allen Smith expressed it very well in 1907:

> The degree of individual freedom and initiative which a community may enjoy is not wholly, or even mainly, a matter of constitutional forms. The actual liberty of the individual may vary greatly without any change in the legal or constitutional organization of society. A political system essentially undemocratic would be much less destructive of individual liberty in a society where the economic life was simple and ownership widely diffused than in a community possessing a wealthy capitalist class on the one hand and an army of wage-earners on the other. . . . Individual liberty in any real sense implies much more than the restriction of governmental authority. In fact, true liberty consists, as we have seen, not in divesting the government of effective power, but in making it an instrument for the unhampered expression and prompt enforcement of public opinion.[96]

Although Smith had sympathizers, their outlook was not yet shared by large numbers of Americans. Progressive reformers generally did, however, acknowledge the desirability of redefining liberty as something more than freedom from physical coercion. Hence the most influential group of Progressives made a modest shift from perceiving liberty as the absence of governmental restraint to re-

---

DeWolfe Howe, ed., *James Bradley Thayer, Oliver Wendell Holmes, and Felix Frankfurter on John Marshall* (Chicago, 1967), 159.

96. Smith, *The Spirit of American Government*, edited by Cushing Strout (1907; reprint, Cambridge, MA, 1965), 306–7.

garding liberty as the conditions that facilitated freedom of opportunity for the populace under an orderly regime. According to the nineteenth-century view, order had been an essential precondition for liberty; and liberty was obliged to function within the constraints of order. The Progressives were moving toward an intellectual inversion—the belief that liberty provides a precondition for order, and a necessary context for order to be both acceptable and meaningful.[97]

Few spokesmen for American ideals invoked the notion of "orderly liberty" more often than Theodore Roosevelt. On many occasions his use of that phrase was vague, banal, or conventionally rhetorical: no more than what public discourse of the day seemed to expect. At times his usage translated into "the priceless union of individual liberty with governmental strength."[98] Two developments, however, were most likely to elicit from TR some sort of specific reference to "ordered liberty" or "liberty under the law": acquisition of the Philippine Islands as a result of the Spanish-American War, and gatherings arranged to commemorate Civil War battles or else the reburial of Union officers at Arlington National Cemetery. Roosevelt might deviate on occasion in order to praise "Union and Liberty," or "liberty and responsibility," or even, once, "democratic liberty"; but the formula to which he returned, time and again, is the one he voiced at Gettysburg on May 30, 1904:

> Some wars have meant the triumph of order over anarchy and licentiousness masquerading as liberty; over tyranny masquerading as order; but this victorious war of ours meant the triumph of both liberty and order, the triumph of orderly liberty, the bestowal of civil rights upon the freed slaves, and at the same time the stern insistence on the supremacy of the national law throughout the length and breadth of the land.[99]

Our new and constitutionally peculiar relationship to the Philippines and Cuba, which aroused that vitriolic controversy over

97. See Tariello, *Reconstruction of American Political Ideology, 1865–1917*, 137, 140–41.
98. See Lewis, ed., *Messages and Speeches of Theodore Roosevelt*, 1:32, 118, 482, 569.
99. For "liberty and order" as TR's constant refrain at Gettysburg, see ibid., 523–25. For similar references in other speeches, ibid., 2, 18, 352, 442, 509, 519, and 627.

whether the U.S. Constitution followed the flag, evoked a related rationale which indicated more particularly how our presence and control would benefit these primitive people just emerging from the dark ages of Spanish tyranny. We would teach them "orderly liberty," the greatest lesson that a civilized society had to offer.[100]

Woodrow Wilson responded to the same question—What rights should be extended to the new dependencies?—in a more restrained manner. His homily on liberty reflected the attitude of large numbers of Americans at the turn of the century. "Liberty is not itself government. In the wrong hands,—in hands unpracticed, undisciplined,—it is incompatible with government. Discipline must precede it,—if necessary, the discipline of being under masters." After asserting that self-control was the prerequisite of liberty, Wilson advised that Filipinos "can have liberty no cheaper than we got it. They must first take the discipline of law, must first love order and instinctively yield to it."[101]

Contemporaries of Wilson and Roosevelt—such widely quoted men as Senators George F. Hoar, Henry Cabot Lodge, Albert J. Beveridge, and jurists like John Marshall Harlan—continued to refer repeatedly to liberty and order. That is not surprising, because they were nineteenth-century men, educated during the Civil War era and imbued with the mood of the later nineteenth century, when articles commonly appeared with titles like "The Lessons of Recent Civil Disorders."[102]

Less easy to explain is the persistence of "ordered liberty" and "liberty and law" as reflex maxims for latter-day Progressives like Charles Evans Hughes and Herbert Hoover. Hoover's apologia and

100. Ibid., 1:179; 2:859; and the quotation in Edmund Morris, *The Rise of Theodore Roosevelt* (New York, 1979), 718.

101. Wilson, "The Ideals of America," *Atlantic Monthly* 90 (December 1902): 730.

102. See, for example, Richard E. Welch, Jr., *George Frisbie Hoar and the Half-Breed Republicans* (Cambridge, MA, 1971), 318; Lodge, *The Democracy of the Constitution* (New York, 1915), 34, 36, 60, 69, 83, 121; John Braeman, *Albert J. Beveridge: American Nationalist* (Chicago, 1971), 231; Paul L. Murphy, "*Near v. Minnesota* in the Context of Historical Developments," *Minnesota Law Review* 66 (November 1981): 124–25; "Lessons of Recent Civil Disorders," *The Forum* 18 (September 1894): 1–19.

credo, *The Challenge to Liberty,* is literally punctuated by the concept of "ordered liberty" as an American ideal, past and present. It would not be inappropriate to call Hoover the last major apostle of ordered liberty, because no one else of his vintage uttered the phrase quite so frequently or believed in it so fervently.[103]

Three different sorts of social phenomena help us to understand the persistence of this obsession during the first third of the twentieth century. To begin with, we must bear in mind the association that many Americans made between cities and moral decay. As established urban areas grew larger, and as towns turned into cities, the level of anxiety rose that social disorder would be unavoidable and potentially devastating. This placed a particular burden upon the developers of resort towns, like Atlantic City, New Jersey, which inspired the morally upright to fear even more that individual liberty might undermine "strict order." Which image would Atlantic City acquire: The great family resort (order)? Or the great pleasure resort (liberty)?[104]

The second social phenomenon involved both the reality and the perception that urban life was not only disorderly but viciously crime-ridden. The growth of crime rates and of police departments to combat crime, especially when the pace of urbanization accelerated after 1865, affected the way people felt about the need to subordinate liberty to order. In recent years we have been informed by social historians that urban disorder actually *decreases* with the passage of time, and that most cities become more orderly as they mature.[105] Although such generalizations go against the grain of

---

103. Charles Evans Hughes, "Liberty and Law," *Report of the 48th Annual Meeting of the American Bar Association* (Baltimore, 1925), 183–99; Hoover, *The Challenge to Liberty* (New York, 1934), 8, 9, 24, 29, 60, 111, 146, 199, 200.

104. See Paul Boyer, *Urban Masses and Moral Order in America, 1820–1920* (Cambridge, MA, 1978), esp. 230–31; Charles E. Funnell, *By the Beautiful Sea* (New York, 1975), 76, 82.

105. John C. Schneider, *Detroit and the Problem of Order, 1830–1880: A Geography of Crime, Riot, and Policing* (Lincoln, NE, 1980); Richard Sennett, "Middle-Class Families and Urban Violence: The Experience of a Chicago Community in the Nineteenth Century," in Stephan Thernstrom and Richard Sennett, eds., *Nineteenth-Century Cities: Essays*

our personal impressions, the statistics bearing upon arrests for disorderly conduct do, in fact, demonstrate a decline. This pattern may help to explain why "liberty and order" began to fade as a popular slogan by the early 1930s.

A third social phenomenon involved the fear of foreign ideologies, such as socialism and anarchism, especially after the 1870s. Many Americans felt that the United States was peculiarly vulnerable to conspiratorial plots because the conditions of freedom were excessive here. Too much liberty could weaken a nation's security. "Liberty and security" even became a contagious code-phrase during the 1920s and 30s.[106]

Obviously, the newer sort of immigrants were a prime source of alien "isms" as well as potential conspirators. Consequently, from 1918 onward the government-prepared handbooks directed at foreigners who sought naturalization and citizenship included an explicit section on "Liberty."

> What is liberty? Why is this a free country? Liberty is the right to be secure in your person and property. It is the right to be governed by law and not by men. This is a government of laws, not a government of men. That is the distinction between this Government and many other Governments. Liberty is not a privilege to do what one pleases, regardless of other people or of other people's property. Liberty is the right to participate in the making of laws and in the selection of the men who hold the offices of the Government. . . . This is a free country because everything the Government does is done in pursuance of law. It is a free country because there is a Constitution which limits the right to make laws, and prohibits the making of

---

in the New Urban History (New Haven, 1969), 386–420; Eric H. Monkkonen, "A Disorderly People? Urban Order in the Nineteenth and Twentieth Centuries," *Journal of American History* 68 (December 1981): 539–59; Stanley K. Schultz, "Temperance Reform in the Antebellum South: Social Control and Urban Order," *South Atlantic Quarterly* 83 (Summer 1984): 323–39.

106. David Brion Davis, ed., *The Fear of Conspiracy: Images of Un-American Subversion from the Revolution to the Present* (Ithaca, 1971), 169–70; *New York Times*, January 8, 1920, p. 16; Hoover, *The Challenge to Liberty*, 196; O. C. Carmichael, "Liberty vs. Security: The Way to Greatness in a Nation," *Vital Speeches of the Day* 4 (August 15, 1938): 669–71.

laws which would infringe upon the natural rights of our people. The Constitution secures these rights in this way.[107]

As a result of all three phenomena, along with the tendency of American constitutional thought to resist change, an outspoken commitment to liberty balanced by order lingered on until the eve of World War II.[108] It was most likely to be invoked in court opinions and on commemorative occasions. When Calvin Coolidge stood at Mount Rushmore in August 1927 to celebrate the initiation of Gutzon Borglum's monumental sculpture of George Washington's head, he offered this accolade to his predecessor: "He stands as the foremost disciple of ordered liberty."[109] Americans returning from a visit to Europe were also likely to comment favorably upon the "orderly freedom" that they found at home (Ludwig Lewisohn in 1934 provides an explicit example).[110]

In addition to Herbert Hoover, however, two contemporaries on the U.S. Supreme Court during the 1930s turned out to be the last spokesmen for ordered liberty. One was Justice Benjamin Cardozo, whose famous opinion in *Palko v. Connecticut* (1937), as we shall see in Part Three, served simultaneously as the culmination of one vision of liberty and the legitimization of another.[111] The second was Chief Justice Charles Evans Hughes, who wrote in 1927 that "it is the function of the Supreme Court to maintain this bal-

---

107. See Raymond F. Crist, *Student's Textbook. A Standard Course of Instruction for Use in the Public Schools of the United States for the Preparation of the Candidate for the Responsibilities of Citizenship* (Washington, D.C., 1921), 28–29.

108. For choice examples of "liberty and order" between 1920 and 1940, see Harry F. Atwood, "The Birthday of Our Constitution," *Constitutional Review* 3 (January 1919): 25; Alpheus T. Mason, *Brandeis: A Free Man's Life* (New York, 1946), 561; *The Bill of Rights Review* 1 (1940): 4, the lead editorial containing a statement of purpose.

109. Quoted in Gilbert C. Fite, *Mount Rushmore* (Norman, OK, 1952), 4. On June 28, 1934, when Charles Hall Davis spoke at Montpelier, Virginia, in honor of James Madison, he referred to "a National Birthright of ordered liberty."

110. Charles C. Alexander, *Here the Country Lies: Nationalism and the Arts in Twentieth-Century America* (Bloomington, 1980), 155. See also Jordan A. Schwartz, *The Speculator: Bernard M. Baruch in Washington, 1917–1965* (Chapel Hill, 1981), 18.

111. See *Palko v. Connecticut*, 302 U.S. 319 (1937).

ance between the constitutional guarantees of liberty and legislative requirements in the interests of the social order." As late as 1941 Hughes would write the opinion for a unanimous Court in a case involving Jehovah's Witnesses who had been convicted in Manchester, New Hampshire, for violating a state law that prohibited holding a parade or procession without obtaining a special license. The Court denied that either the right of assembly or the right to discuss public questions in public places had been abridged. "Civil liberties," Hughes wrote, "as guaranteed by the Constitution, imply the existence of an organized society maintaining public order without which liberty itself would be lost in the excesses of unrestrained abuses."[112]

Along with Cardozo, however, Hughes also understood that major changes in the concept of liberty were taking place, and that a reformulation quietly begun at the turn of the century would soon lead American social and political thought to a new plateau. When Hughes presented his presidential address to the American Bar Association in 1925, he gave it a conventional title, "Liberty and Law." He touched the conventional bases, and bowed in the direction of "a well-ordered freedom." He went on to observe, though, that "liberty is today a broader conception than ever before."[113] The accuracy of that comment, and the reasons why, will be the subject of Part Three.

112. Hughes, *The Supreme Court of the United States: Its Foundation, Methods and Achievements* (New York, 1928), 162–63; and *Cox et al. v. New Hampshire*, 312 U.S. 569 (1941), the quotation at 574. See also Gerald T. Dunne, *Hugo Black and the Judicial Revolution* (New York 1977), 258.

113. Hughes, "Liberty and Law," 183–99, esp. 185 and 187.

13. "Emancipation Proclamation," oil on canvas by A. A. Lamb (1863 or later). Note the shackles, fetters, and bullwhip on the ground. The flag has "Liberty to All" stitched on its field of blue. (Courtesy, National Gallery of Art [Garbisch Collection], Washington, D.C.)

14. Liberty weathervane, copper with a verdigris patina (ca. 1864). The flag has thirty-five stars. West Virginia was admitted in 1863 as the thirty-fifth state, and Nevada in 1864 as the thirty-sixth. (Courtesy, Marna Anderson Gallery, New York City.)

15. Liberty weathervane, gilded metal (nineteenth century). Many patriotic objects continued to show only thirteen stars throughout the nineteenth century, even though additional states had been added. (Courtesy, National Gallery of Art, Washington, D.C.)

16. Liberty, a seated figure made of carved and painted wood by Eliodoro Parete, an Italian, in Anawalt, West Virginia (after 1863). Note that "Liberty" is carved into her tiara. (Courtesy, National Gallery of Art, Washington, D.C.)

BARSQUALDI'S STATUE
LIBERTY FRIGHTENING THE WORLD.
BEDBUGS ISLAND, N.Y. HARBOR.
(Only Authorized Edition.)

17. "Barsqualdi's Statue, Liberty Frightening the World," a lithograph made by Thomas Worth for Currier and Ives (1884). The Statue of Liberty has often been used in advertising, but infrequently for purposes of satire. This caricature was directed at corruption in the administration of New York Harbor. (Courtesy, Library of Congress, Washington, D.C.)

18. Liberty, a watercolor rendering by Elizabeth Fairchild (1938) of a ship's figurehead of wood and sheet iron, probably made in Massachusetts during the later 1860s, originally painted light gray. Following the original, Liberty's bodice, belt, and wrist-bands are lined with gold. Her liberty cap and laurel-leaf crown are gilded. (Courtesy, Index of American Design, National Gallery of Art, Washington, D.C.)

19. Liberty, a watercolor rendering by Frances Cohen (1939) of a late-nineteenth-century weathervane made of sheet copper and drawn brass tubing. The original was found in Penobscot Valley, Maine. (Courtesy, Index of American Design, National Gallery of Art, Washington, D.C.)

20. "Ms Liberty at High Tide" (1979), Madison, Wisconsin. This work was constructed in February 1979 on ice-covered Lake Mendota near the University of Wisconsin Memorial Union. The Wisconsin Student Association provided funding. Five sculptors and fifty volunteers assembled the project. Materials included a plywood substructure, fiberglass resin, styrofoam (the head), and papier-mâché (the arm and torch). (Courtesy, the University of Wisconsin News Service.)

21. "The Other Freedom," charcoal on paper, by LiFran E. Fort (1985), an artist who teaches at Fisk University in Nashville, Tennessee. (From the collection and with the permission of the artist.)

22. Approaching Liberty, Tioga County, Pennsylvania. This town began as a blockhouse supply depot, built in 1792 when a road was constructed from Trout Run to Blossburg, Pennsylvania, and then to Painted Post, New York. There are towns named "Liberty" in Indiana, Kentucky, Mississippi, Missouri, New York, North Carolina, South Carolina, Tennessee, and Texas. There are many others called Libertyville, Libertytown, Liberty Hill, Liberty Center, Liberty Mills, and Liberty Grove.

Part Three

*

Liberty, Justice, and Equality in Twentieth-Century America

"No one shall be deprived of liberty without due process of law. Here is a concept of the greatest generality. Yet it is put before the courts *en bloc*. Liberty is not defined. Its limits are not mapped and charted. How shall they be known? Does liberty mean the same thing for successive generations? May restraints that were arbitrary yesterday be useful and rational and therefore lawful tomorrow? I have no doubt that the answer to these questions must be yes. There were times in our judicial history when the answer might have been no. Liberty was conceived of at first as something static and absolute. . . . Gradually, however, though not without frequent protest and intermittent movements backward, a new conception of the significance of constitutional limitations in the domain of individual liberty, emerged to recognition and to dominance."

Benjamin N. Cardozo, *The Nature of the Judicial Process* (1921), 76–78.

"Government without liberty is a curse; but, on the other hand, liberty without government is far from being a blessing."

John Jay to George Washington, September 21, 1788.

Viewed with the help of hindsight, American conceptions of liberty clearly underwent a transformation between 1932 and 1937. When Franklin D. Roosevelt campaigned for the presidency in 1932, he was still a captive of the basic nineteenth-century formula. As he declared at San Francisco in the famous Commonwealth Club speech: "Individual liberty and individual happiness mean nothing unless both are ordered in the sense that one man's meat is not another man's poison." And when the widely respected Senator William E. Borah of Idaho, a Progressive turned conservative, spoke on "Constitutional Government" in Washington, D.C., on September 16, 1937, he praised the Constitution because it had "held together people of all climes, races and faiths in ordered liberty, which gives freedom to all who come within its jurisdiction, which makes the people sovereign and public officials their agents. . . ."[1]

Justice Benjamin Cardozo's opinion for the Supreme Court in the much-cited case of *Palko v. Connecticut* (1937) has customarily been viewed as the most succinct and influential formulation of "ordered liberty" as a judicial concept. Without rejecting the validity of that assumption, I would like to suggest that Cardozo's concerns in writing that opinion were broader than we have recognized; and on that account the case is transitional in a highly symptomatic and revealing way. Let's consider the circumstances of the case, the words from Cardozo's opinion that are so frequently quoted, and then two passages that are normally neglected.

The Connecticut legislature passed a law permitting appeals involving criminal cases to be made by the State where it felt that a case had been lost because of a procedural error. When the defendant in a particular murder case was sentenced to death as a result of such a retrial, however, he appealed on the grounds that

1. Roosevelt, Campaign Address on Progressive Government at the Commonwealth Club, San Francisco, September 23, 1932, in Samuel I. Rosenman, ed., *The Public Papers and Addresses of Franklin D. Roosevelt* (New York, 1938), 1:755; Borah, "Constitutional Government," *Vital Speeches of the Day* 4 (October 15, 1937): 5.

he had been subjected to double jeopardy for the same crime, and that his right to due process under the Fourteenth Amendment had been denied. Cardozo's analysis of the episode seems cautious in several respects. He refused to apply the entire Bill of Rights to the states, and specifically that phrase in the Fifth Amendment that reads: "nor shall any person be subject for the same offense to be twice put in jeopardy of life or limb." Cardozo acknowledged that "the right to trial by jury and the immunity from prosecution except as the result of an indictment may have value and importance. Even so," he added, "they are not of the very essence of a scheme of ordered liberty." He therefore upheld the right of a state to conduct a trial free from legal error.[2]

Elsewhere in the opinion, however, Cardozo acknowledged that numerous and varied applications of the Fourteenth Amendment had resulted in a reinterpretation of the meaning of liberty: "The domain of liberty withdrawn by the Fourteenth Amendment from encroachment by the states, has been enlarged by latter-day judgments to include liberty of the mind as well as liberty of action. . . . Liberty is something more than exemption from physical restraint. . . ." He even conceded that in many cases "immunities that are valid as against the federal government by force of the specific pledges of particular amendments have been found to be implicit in the concept of ordered liberty, and thus, through the Fourteenth Amendment, become valid as against the states."[3]

The two references to "ordered liberty" are more closely associated with Cardozo's name than any other words he ever wrote. That is the phrase that caused the case to be cited frequently. Nevertheless, there is a second concept that Cardozo also used twice in his *Palko* opinion, one not usually quoted because it occurs in that part of the opinion where he is exploring the realm of possible outcomes, and because it did not have the judicial timbre that "ordered liberty" did. Almost at the outset of his explication, Cardozo

2. *Palko v. Connecticut*, 302 U.S. 319, (1937), the quotation at 324–25.
3. Ibid., 325, 327.

commented that "the process of absorption whereby some of the privileges and immunities guaranteed by the federal bill of rights have been brought within the Fourteenth Amendment, has had its source in the belief that neither liberty nor justice would exist if they were sacrificed." And once again, at the end of his opinion, Cardozo speculated whether the double jeopardy to which the defendant had been subjected violated "those fundamental principles of liberty and justice which lie at the base of all our civil and political institutions?"[4]

Cardozo, a man of the highest integrity and great compassion, was able to answer, in this instance, No. Nonetheless, it is noteworthy that although he had used the phrase "ordered liberty" twice, he had also used "liberty and justice" at the beginning as well as at the close of his exegesis. The second time he did so, moreover, he was actually quoting from the 1926 case of *Hebert v. Louisiana.*[5] The linkage between liberty and justice, which had been developing for decades, came into its own in 1937–38. Elsewhere Cardozo asserted that freedom of speech and thought are "the matrix, the indispensable condition, of nearly every other form of freedom. . . . Neither liberty nor justice would exist if they were sacrificed."[6]

On Constitution Day (September 17) in 1937, the President of Rutgers University told those who had gathered for a special convocation that "the same principles of human justice, human liberty and rights of the individual which held good in 1787 hold good today." When the Supreme Court upheld the Wagner Act and the National Labor Relations Board in 1937, students of American jurisprudence remarked that the concept of liberty had been revolutionized. It had shifted from a negative notion that restricted

---

4. Ibid., 320, 328. Cardozo had foreshadowed his concern for liberty and justice ten years earlier when he presented the Carpentier Fund Lectures at Columbia University. See *The Paradoxes of Legal Science* (New York, 1928), 31–52, 94–132.

5. *Hebert et al. v. Louisiana*, 272 U.S. 312 (1926), esp. 316.

6. Quoted in Herman C. Pritchett, "The Judicial Revolution and American Democracy," in Thomas R. Ford, ed., *The Revolutionary Theme in Contemporary America* (Lexington, KY, 1965), 71.

legislative power to a positive one that called for legislative action to enhance the rights of ordinary citizens. During the later 1930s, liberty and justice began to be lifted above ordered liberty in the American system of values.[7]

Because liberty and order had been the predominant formula for such a long time, however, public uncertainty was discernible until the transformation had time to be established and applied. In April 1938, for example, James M. Landis, the Dean of Harvard's Law School, presented a talk on ABC radio entitled "Liberty as an Evolutionary Idea: A Sense of Confusion Prevails." In it he tried to explain the intellectual revolution in progress:

> If we try to define for today, even in a tentative fashion, the newer ideals that in a short space of a time have clustered about the conception of liberty, a more expansive charter of rights seems to have come into being. Instead of a philosophy that rests upon the belief that only good could come from the absence of restraint and that the essence of freedom lay in that fact, to-day's society seems to build upon a faith that it is the function of our economy to assure certain minimum claims to individuals. . . . Clearly the effect of seeking to realize this newer conception of liberty has erased a great deal of the old, familiar economic pattern of our society. . . . It may be that as important as administrative justice are the implications to judicial justice of the marked tendency of this century to turn the new liberties over to administrative agencies for safe-keeping. . . . In the place of the theory that liberties would come as a by-product from the unhampered and undirected play of economic forces, concern now manifests itself toward the attainment of these liberties as the direct objectives of governmental action. A sense of confusion today dominates the political and economic scene. Partly this flows

---

7. *New York Times*, September 18, 1937, p. 2; Edward S. Corwin, *Court Over Constitution: A Study of Judicial Review as an Instrument of Popular Government* (Princeton, 1938), 124–25. "From a purely *negative* concept restrictive of legislative power liberty thus becomes a *positive* concept calling for legislative implementation and protection. Or, to put the same thought from a somewhat different angle, whereas 'liberty' as a constitutional value has been usually thought of in the past as something capable of being endangered only by government, it is now recognized as being often in danger from other forces and to need the protection of government against them. The Court thus recognizes the force of Burke's statement, 'Liberty, when men act in bodies, is power'—a statement which is equally true for capital and for labor."

from the fact that too little delineation of our political ideology has taken place. . . . Partly the existing confusion flows from an unwillingness to accept the implications entailed by the new liberties, a longing for a staid but dead past.[8]

Neither liberty and justice nor the context supplied by Landis was entirely new in 1937–38. Protection for the individual against government and the opinions of an impulsive majority had been discussed, albeit intermittently, for a very long time. A belief in government intervention to improve the economy on behalf of both private persons and the society as a whole has credentials that harken back to Alexander Hamilton's stewardship as Secretary of the Treasury. And if we ransack the records of American thought, the concept of liberty and justice turns up in some highly unexpected texts: even ones by Fisher Ames, David Jayne Hill, and Herbert Hoover, for example.[9] Nevertheless, the concept appears with much greater frequency after 1937, and with expanded meaning as well as enhanced priority in relation to liberty and authority, property, and order. Be that as it may, we are obliged to glance back at the usages and applications of liberty and justice between 1787 and 1937 before proceeding to the most recent half-century in our history and the implications of liberty for our own time.

The concept of justice was not entirely absent from the seventeenth- and eighteenth-century "spirit of the age," but neither was it common. Explicit ties between liberty and justice appeared even less

8. Landis, "Liberty as an Evolutionary Idea," *Vital Speeches of the Day* 4 (June 1, 1938): 488–89.

9. See Ames to Timothy Pickering, December 22, 1806, in Seth Ames, ed., *The Life and Works of Fisher Ames* (Boston, 1854), 1:380; editorial, "For Constitutional Clubs," *North American Review* 198 (December 1913): 764; Hill, "The Crisis in American Constitutionalism," in Hill, *Americanism, What It Is* (New York, 1916), 82; Hill, "The Assault on the Constitution and the Courts," *Constitutional Review* 9 (January 1925): 17; Hoover, *The Challenge to Liberty* (New York, 1934), 2, 100.

often. The writings of John Locke, for example, could easily be used to bolster arguments on behalf of liberty and property, even liberty and order; but not liberty and justice. Despite some ill-informed statements to the contrary, the problem of justice did interest Locke; but it is largely absent from the *Two Treatises of Government*, and eighteenth-century Americans did not connect questions involving justice with Lockean justifications.[10]

In 1721 "Cato's Letters" remarked that "by the Establishment of Liberty, a due Distribution of Property and an Equal Distribution of Justice is established and secured"; yet such comments were uncommon among the "Real Whigs" and rare among mainstream Whigs. When liberty and justice were mentioned at all, it was as likely to occur in a reference to the situation in Poland as in one to Britain or her colonies.[11] Toward the end of the century Edmund Burke did, as we have seen, occasionally connect liberty with justice. He wrote in 1789 that "whenever a separation is made between Liberty and Justice, neither is, in my opinion, safe." But statements of that sort were unusual; and M. J. C. Vile is fundamentally correct when he observes that the concept of social justice did not really emerge as a normative aspect of political thought until the twentieth century.[12]

Those who are familiar with American culture during the la-

10. See Nathan Tarcov, *Locke's Education for Liberty* (Chicago, 1984), 145–53; H. T. Dickinson, *Liberty and Property: Political Ideology in Eighteenth-Century Britain* (New York, 1977), 65, 68, 70; John Locke, *Two Treatises of Government*, edited by Peter Laslett (Cambridge, 1967), 84.

11. David L. Jacobson, ed., *The English Libertarian Heritage: From the Writings of John Trenchard and Thomas Gordon in "The Independent Whig" and "Cato's Letters"* (Indianapolis, 1965), 138; Richard Price to William Rix, March 23, 1776, in Bernard Peach and D. O. Thomas, eds., *The Correspondence of Richard Price* (Durham, NC, 1983), 1:243–44; J. A. W. Gunn, *Beyond Liberty and Property: The Process of Self-Recognition in Eighteenth-Century Political Thought* (Kingston and Montreal, 1983), 240–41.

12. Burke to Charles-Jean-François Depont (November 1789), in Alfred Cobban and Robert A. Smith, eds., *The Correspondence of Edmund Burke* (Chicago, 1967), 6:42; Vile, *Constitutionalism and the Separation of Powers* (Oxford, 1967), 294–314. There is an unusual painting at the Louvre in Paris by Henri de Favannes (1668–1752) entitled "Le triomphe de la justice."

ter eighteenth century might wish to dispute that assertion. Even though the single-sentence Preamble to the U.S. Constitution does not explicitly link liberty and justice, it does specify among the purposes in establishing the document a desire to "establish justice" and to "secure the blessings of liberty to ourselves and our posterity." From time to time American leaders have reminded their auditors and correspondents that liberty and justice both appear in the Preamble. Frederick Douglass did so in 1850, for instance, and Franklin D. Roosevelt in 1934.[13]

During the Constitutional Convention held at Philadelphia in 1787, James Madison made a point of including "the security of private rights, and the steady dispensation of Justice" among the primary objects of government, an assertion that he elaborated upon in *Federalist* number 51: "Justice is the end of government. It is the end of civil society. It ever has been, and ever will be pursued, until it be obtained, or until liberty be lost in the pursuit."[14] We also encounter an occasional advocate of ratification as well as some Antifederalists employing the phrase. On November 2, 1787, an essayist in the *Connecticut Gazette* called the Constitution "an ark for the preservation of the justice and liberties of the world"; yet six days later Cincinnatus II indicated alarm "when I see these Doctors of our constitution cutting in twain this sacred shield of public liberty and justice."[15]

13. See Staughton Lynd, "The Abolitionist Critique of the United States Constitution," in Martin Duberman, ed., *The Antislavery Vanguard: New Essays on the Abolitionists* (Princeton, 1965), 211; Roosevelt to the American Judicature Society, May 9, 1934, in Rosenman, ed., *Public Papers and Addresses of Franklin D. Roosevelt*, 3:218. See also Gerald W. Johnson, "When to Build a Barricade" (1938) in Johnson, *America-Watching: Perspectives in the Course of an Incredible Century* (Owings Mills, MD, 1976), 114.

14. Madison speaking on June 6, 1787, in Max Farrand, ed., *The Records of the Federal Convention of 1787* (rev. ed.: New Haven, 1937), 1:134; Jacob E. Cooke, ed., *The Federalist* (Middletown, CT, 1961), 352. See also section 15 of the Virginia Bill of Rights (1776).

15. Frank I. Schechter, "The Early History of the Tradition of the Constitution," *American Political Science Review* 9 (November 1915): 724; John P. Kaminski and Gaspare J. Saladino, eds., *Commentaries on the Constitution, Public and Private, November 8 to December 17, 1787*, vol. 14 of *The Documentary History of the Ratification of the Constitution* (Madison, 1983), 14.

The appearance of that phrase in public discourse over the next two decades, however, was rare. When William Rawle, a Philadelphia lawyer, invoked it in 1793 he actually had the "public acts" of post-revolutionary France in mind. When George Warner acknowledged in 1797 that "a sense of Liberty and of Justice prevails among us," he soon followed with the predictable incantation of "order and fair liberty." In 1806 the highest court of Massachusetts did express its concern for "civil liberty, natural justice, and the spirit of our constitution and laws."[16] The infrequency of such language, along with the lack of any standardized slogan, would seem to support (about as well as negative evidence can) Francis W. Coker's generalization that the founders "talked in terms of social utility and power, not of individual liberty and justice."[17]

This pattern persisted throughout the course of the next two generations, from the 1820s until the 1880s. Apart from some abolitionist orators, who were understandably fond of the phrase "Liberty and Justice" and wished to preserve the Union "by doing justice and securing liberty to all,"[18] the only prominent public figure who elaborated the concept was John Quincy Adams in the context of his *Discourse* for the Golden Jubilee of the Constitution in 1839. Even so, Adams's only statement actually connecting liberty with justice (in 120 pages of text) was really just a précis of the Preamble itself. Otherwise he emphasized justice as a primary purpose of government without making any reference to liberty at all. He insisted, for example, that justice involved "the constant and per-

16. Rawle is quoted in Charles Warren, *The Supreme Court in United States History* (Boston, 1922), 1:106; G. J. Warner, *Means for the Preservation of Public Liberty. An Oration Delivered in the New Dutch Church, on the Fourth of July, 1797* . . . (New York, 1797), 10, 19; Edward S. Corwin, *Liberty Against Government: The Rise, Flowering and Decline of a Famous Juridical Concept* (Baton Rouge, 1948), 75–76.

17. Coker, "American Traditions Concerning Property and Liberty," *American Political Science Review* 30 (February 1936): 5.

18. See Lynd, "Abolitionist Critique of the United States Constitution," 211; Wendell Phillips quoted in George M. Fredrickson, *The Inner Civil War: Northern Intellectuals and the Crisis of the Union* (New York, 1965), 128; and Morton Keller, *Affairs of State: Public Life in Late Nineteenth Century America* (Cambridge, MA, 1977), 218.

petual will of securing to every one his *right,* [and] includes the whole duty of man in the social institutions of society, toward his neighbor. To the establishment of this JUSTICE, the joint and harmonious co-operation of the legislative and executive departments was required. . . ."[19]

Otherwise the theme can best be described as highly sporadic and incompletely articulated. In Abraham Lincoln's first inaugural address, for instance, he mentions justice three times in a single paragraph without once referring to liberty. Lincoln repeatedly pledged himself, moreover, not to disturb the institution of slavery in any place where it legally existed.[20] Chancellor Kent, in his *Commentaries on American Law* (1826–30), had remarked that liberty "depends essentially upon the structure of government, [and] the administration of justice," an emphasis that appeared occasionally during the nineteenth century.[21]

The only other noteworthy trend took the form of a modest internationalization of the theme during the decade following the American Civil War. One writer proclaimed in 1867, for example, that "the great theoretic principles of universal justice and universal liberty are fully understood, and it is to be hoped, firmly and forever established." When the Franco-Prussian War broke out in 1870, most Americans tended to be pro-German. *Harper's Weekly* declared that "the cause of Germany is that of liberty and justice," thereby

19. Adams, *The Jubilee of the Constitution. A Discourse Delivered at the Request of the New-York Historical Society . . .* (New York, 1839), 47, 70, 72, 73, 106.

20. Roy P. Basler, ed., *The Collected Works of Abraham Lincoln* (New Brunswick, NJ, 1953), 4:262–71, esp. 270. John Wilkes Booth, Lincoln's assassin, wrote a sealed letter of explanation and left it with his brother-in-law for safekeeping. It remained unopened until it was discovered after the assassination. The fourth paragraph began with this sentence: "People of the North, to hate tyranny, to love liberty and justice, to strike at wrong and oppression, was the teaching of our fathers." Quoted in James W. Clarke, *American Assassins: The Darker Side of Politics* (Princeton, 1982), 30.

21. Kent is quoted in Corwin, *Liberty Against Government,* 78; see also Warren, *Supreme Court in United States History,* 3:159, 295, quoting the *Springfield Republican* in 1867 and Justice Stephen J. Field in 1885; Rutherford B. Hayes, fourth annual message to Congress, December 6, 1880, in James D. Richardson, ed., *A Compilation of the Messages and Papers of the Presidents, 1789–1897* (Washington, D.C., 1896–99), 7:604.

bonding German goals with American values. In 1876 President Grant issued a Centennial proclamation that the United States had been able to "fulfill the purpose of its founders in offering an asylum to the people of every race, securing civil and religious liberty to all within its borders, and meting out to every individual alike justice and equality before the law."[22]

Between 1884 and 1916, however, a gradual but significant transformation commenced. In 1884, when the Supreme Court issued its opinions pertaining to a murder case known as *Hurtado v. California*, the conflicting views constituted a full-scale dialogue that began to alter the operative meaning of liberty and justice in constitutional law. Justice Stanley Matthews, writing for the majority, stated that the words "due process of law" in the Fourteenth Amendment did not necessarily require an indictment by a grand jury to validate a murder prosecution by a state. In explaining his line of reasoning, however, Matthews referred no fewer than three times to "those fundamental principles of liberty and justice which lie at the base of all our civil and political institutions."

> In this country written constitutions were deemed essential to protect the rights and liberties of the people against the encroachments of power delegated to their governments, and the provisions of Magna Charta were incorporated into Bills of Rights. . . . It necessarily happened, therefore, that as these broad and general maxims of liberty and justice held in our system a different place and performed a different function from their position and office in English constitutional history and law, they would receive and justify a corresponding and more comprehensive interpretation.[23]

22. H. T. Blake, "Judge Farrar on the Constitution," *The New Englander* 26 (October 1967), 739; Keller, *Affairs of State*, 87; Richardson, ed., *Messages and Papers of the Presidents*, 7:397. See also President Arthur's proclamation of October 25, 1882, designating November 30 as a day of public thanksgiving. "The blessings demanding our gratitude are numerous and varied. For the peace and amity which subsist between this Republic and all the nations of the world; for the freedom from internal discord and violence; for the increasing friendship between the different sections of the land; for liberty, justice and constitutional government. . . ." Richardson, ed., *Messages and Papers of the Presidents*, 8:123.

23. *Hurtado v. California*, 110 U.S. 516 (1884), the quotations at 531–32, 535. Extracts

Justice John Marshall Harlan dissented, however, and supported Hurtado's claim that the lack of a grand jury indictment did indeed deprive him of due process of law. (Hurtado had been brought to trial after a "mere" examination by a magistrate, in accordance with California's constitution.) The essential thrust of Harlan's lengthy dissent addressed the issue, What is required to provide "liberty and justice"? and invoked that phrase no fewer than six times. He accused the majority of his brethren of being more concerned about the maintenance of order than with following procedures requisite for the achievement of justice. "The Court, in this case, while conceding that the requirement of due process of law protects the fundamental principles of liberty and justice, adjudges, in effect, that an immunity or right, recognized at the common law to be essential to personal security . . . is, yet, not a fundamental principle in governments established . . . to secure to the citizen liberty and justice, and, therefore, is not involved in that due process of law required in proceedings conducted under the sanction of a State."[24]

A similar judicial episode occurred twenty-four years later in the case of *Twining v. State of New Jersey* (1908), when Justice William H. Moody, writing for the Court, concluded that exemption from compulsory self-incrimination in state courts was not mandated by any part of the Federal Constitution. Although this interpretation perpetuated the belief that, despite the Fourteenth Amendment's due process clause, the Bill of Rights did not apply in state courts, the Supreme Court had undergone an important shift simply by raising the question: "Is it a fundamental principle of liberty and justice which inheres in the very idea of free government?" For the moment, however, the Court seemed satisfied with Moody's rationale: "The power of the people of the States to make and alter

---

appear in Stanley I. Kutler, ed., *The Supreme Court and the Constitution: Readings in American Constitutional History* (2nd ed.: New York, 1977), 193–96.

   24. *Hurtado v. California* 110 U.S. 516 (1884), at 546, 549, and the quotation at 557–58. See also Corwin, *Liberty Against Government*, 134–35, 167, for historical context.

their laws at pleasure is the greatest security for liberty and justice, this Court has said in *Hurtado v. California.*"²⁵

Justice Harlan dissented once again, deeply disturbed by his brethren's seemingly casual lack of concern that their decision might facilitate future intrusions upon the individual's right against self-incrimination. By the earliest years of the twentieth century, however, signals began to appear outside of the Supreme Court to suggest that new priorities were beginning to surface. On September 8, 1892, for instance, a juvenile magazine called *Youth's Companion,* published in Boston, printed a pledge of allegiance to the flag. Apparently written by one Francis Bellamy, a young assistant editor, it included the phrase, long since familiar, "with liberty and justice for all." Although that pledge was not officially adopted by Congress as *the* pledge until 1942, it caught on quickly, was widely reprinted and adopted for use on patriotic occasions. A slogan had started to catch the nation's fancy.²⁶

A commitment to social justice emerged simultaneously as one of the more prominent characteristics of Progressive thought, and provided (as a kind of dividend) fresh attention to the concept of liberty and justice.²⁷ When Theodore Roosevelt addressed the Iroquois Club in Chicago on May 10, 1905, he insisted that a consensus existed among "all good Americans" on at least one matter: "They are all one in the conviction, in the firm determination that this country shall remain in the future as it has been in the past, a country of liberty and justice expressed through the forms of

25. *Twining v. State of New Jersey,* 211 U.S. 78 (1908), at 99, 106, 111, and 114. For historical context, see John E. Semonche, *Charting the Future: The Supreme Court Responds to a Changing Society, 1890–1920* (Westport, CT, 1978), 225–27.

26. "Pledge of Allegiance to the U.S. Flag," *Encyclopaedia Britannica* (Chicago, 1970), 18:42. In 1900 one of William Jennings Bryan's campaign posters for the presidency read: "The Issue – 1900: Liberty, Justice, Humanity."

27. See Harold U. Faulkner, *The Quest for Social Justice, 1898–1914* (New York, 1931); J. Allen Smith, *The Spirit of American Government,* edited by Cushing Strout (1907; reprint, Cambridge, MA, 1965), 297, 301; Charles Evans Hughes, *The Supreme Court of the United States: Its Foundation, Methods and Achievements* (New York, 1928), 241. Hughes's final two chapters are entitled "Liberty, Property and Social Justice."

law." In subsequent speeches and essays Roosevelt revealed a shift in his emphasis from ordered liberty "toward a juster and fairer life system." In somewhat muted form, Woodrow Wilson's pronouncements underwent a comparable change.[28]

During the quarter-century that followed 1912, liberty and justice appeared with growing frequency in public discourse, journalism, scholarship, and popular education. The phrase gradually became commonplace in student orations and in civics textbooks for secondary school students. In 1917 one expert felt comfortable making this sort of cosmic pronouncement: "The history of Magna Carta in America has a meaning far deeper than the influence of a single constitutional document. . . . The world-wide diffusion of those ideals of liberty and justice deserves to be studied in its entirety as a vast historical process."[29]

Both the idealism that accompanied our participation in World War I as well as the critical pessimism stimulated by the Great Depression helped to encourage this general trend in American thought. In 1917, for example, the French leader Léon Blum welcomed America's entry into the war in support of the allies by proclaiming that "our victory will be the emancipation and reconciliation of men through Liberty and Justice," a declaration that received sympathetic responses in the United States.[30] One of the central themes in Reinhold Niebuhr's influential book, *Moral Man and Immoral Society* (1932), found expression in his belief that "equal justice is the most rational ultimate objective for society."[31]

28. Theodore Roosevelt, *Presidential Addresses and State Papers* (New York, 1910), 4:374; Roosevelt, "Democratic Ideals," *The Outlook* 105 (November 15, 1913): 595; Wilson, *The New Freedom* (New York, 1912), ch. 9, "Benevolence, or Justice?"

29. See H. Arnold Bennett, *The Constitution in School and College* (New York, 1935), 84, 180; George Bryan Logan, Jr., *Liberty in the Modern World* (Chapel Hill, 1928), 6, 26; H. D. Hazeltine, "The Influence of Magna Carta on American Constitutional Development," *Columbia Law Review* 17 (January 1917): 33.

30. Joel Colton, *Léon Blum: Humanist in Politics* (New York, 1966), 41.

31. Niebuhr, *Moral Man and Immoral Society: A Study in Ethics and Politics* (New York, 1932), 231–34. See also Studs Terkel, *Hard Times: An Oral History of the Great Depression* (Avon ed.: New York, 1971), 141.

Legal and constitutional issues that arose during these years also shaped the reorientation of American attitudes toward liberty. As early as 1912, four years before Woodrow Wilson appointed him to the Supreme Court, Louis D. Brandeis had decided that the customary meaning of liberty and property sorely needed redefinition. His dissenting opinion in *Gilbert v. Minnesota* (1920), moreover, made a fresh and compelling case for freedom of speech and thought. In that instance the Court sustained a state law punishing speech that aimed to discourage enlistment in the military services. Brandeis argued that laws of that sort inhibited the right of an American citizen to discuss such federal functions as the war power.[32]

In 1927 the protracted case of *Whitney v. California* (it started in 1919), concerning organizational efforts on behalf of the Communist Labor Party of California, provoked a concurring opinion from Brandeis that served as a form of dissent by effectively calling for a reassessment of all the conventional notions pertaining to liberty. Brandeis did so, moreover, by invoking the revolutionaries of 1776 and the founders of the nation:

> All fundamental rights comprised within the term liberty are protected by the Federal Constitution from invasion by the States. . . . Those who won our independence by revolution were not cowards. They did not fear political change. They did not exalt order at the cost of liberty. . . . Only an emergency can justify repression. Such must be the rule if authority is to be reconciled with freedom. Such, in my opinion, is the command of the Constitution.[33]

In 1923 the Supreme Court found unconstitutional a state law that prohibited the teaching of any modern language other than

32. Alpheus T. Mason, *Brandeis: A Free Man's Life* (New York, 1946), 579; Paul L. Murphy, "*Near v. Minnesota* in the Context of Historical Developments," *Minnesota Law Review* 66 (November 1981): 113–16, 141–45, 151–53; Alfred H. Kelly, Winfred A. Harbison, and Herman Belz, *The American Constitution: Its Origins and Development* (6th ed.: New York, 1983), 532–33.

33. *Whitney v. California*, 274 U.S. 357 (1927), the quotations at 373 and 377. When

English to children who had not yet completed the eighth grade. This superficially minor case, *Meyer v. State of Nebraska*, elicited not only one of the fullest statements concerning liberty ever to come from the Court, but one that would also be quoted for more than half a century whenever the justices had to explain their understanding of "liberty" in the due process clause of the Fourteenth Amendment. Justice James C. McReynolds — not ordinarily regarded as a wild-eyed radical — wrote the Court's opinion, which found that the state law had infringed liberties that were protected by the Fourteenth Amendment:

> The spirit of America is liberty and toleration — the disposition to allow each person to live his own life in his own way, unhampered by unreasonable and arbitrary restrictions. . . . The term [liberty] has received much consideration. . . . Without doubt, it denotes not merely freedom from bodily restraint but also the right of the individual to contract, to engage in any of the common occupations of life, to acquire useful knowledge, to marry, to establish a home and bring up children, to worship God according to the dictates of his own conscience, and generally to enjoy those privileges long recognized . . . as essential to the orderly pursuit of happiness by free men.[34]

Another important case, decided in 1926, would also be frequently cited in later decisions and helped to make "liberty and justice" an integral part of the parlance of American constitutionalism. When Louisiana passed a law (during nationwide Prohibition) making it a criminal offense to manufacture intoxicating beverages, defendants claimed that they would be subjected to double jeopardy if they were prosecuted under both state and Federal legislation. Willis Van Devanter, writing for a unanimous bench, upheld the

---

the Supreme Court explicitly overruled *Whitney* in 1969, its decision was based upon Brandeis's reasoning in 1927. See Alan Barth, *Prophets With Honor: Great Dissents and Great Dissenters in the Supreme Court* (New York, 1974), 170 and n. 10.

34. *Meyer v. State of Nebraska*, 262 U.S. 390 (1923), the quotations at 392 and 399. This lengthy extract from *Meyer* would be quoted much later in two controversial cases: one involving abortion (*Roe et al. v. Wade*, 410 U.S. 113 [1973], at 153, 168–69), and the other the rehiring of college teachers (by the University of Wisconsin) (*Board of Regents of State Colleges et al. v. Roth*, 408 U.S. 564 [1972], at 572).

Supreme Court of Louisiana and rejected the defendants' plea. "The due process of law clause in the Fourteenth Amendment [requires] . . . that state action, whether through one agency or another, shall be consistent with the fundamental principles of liberty and justice which lie at the base of all our civil and political institutions."[35] Upholding the principle of federalism, in this instance, meant sustaining the sovereignty of separate spheres. Van Devanter did so in the name of liberty and justice.

In that same year, 1926, the prominent constitutional historian Charles Warren published a benchmark essay concerning a problem that was just then moving toward solution. Warren criticized the Supreme Court for steadily broadening its interpretation of the language of the due process clause in the Fourteenth Amendment. He complained that the concept of liberty had received considerably expanded implications since the close of the nineteenth century, called it "an especially convenient vehicle into which to pack all kinds of rights," lamented the fact that the due process clause lacked a "definite meaning," and asserted that the freedom of state legislatures had been sacrificed to a new and unjustified notion of "liberty" for the individual.[36] Warren had written many influential essays during his career; but in this instance, History was about to overtake him. He had described extremely well the dominant tendency of the generation that followed 1885. Within a few years, however, the "new" liberty of which he complained in 1926 would be replaced by a still newer one.

Throughout the 1920s a delicate equilibrium prevailed between the advocates of a reoriented definition of liberty—or at least a shift in emphasis—and apologists for the traditional points of view. In 1916 Learned Hand published a widely noticed essay entitled

35. *Hebert et al. v. Louisiana*, 272 U.S. 312 (1926), the quotation at 312–13.
36. Warren, "The New 'Liberty' Under the Fourteenth Amendment," *Harvard Law Review* 39 (February 1926): 431–65.

"The Speech of Justice" in which he referred contemptuously to the notion of "ordered liberty" and urged that it be replaced by a revitalized quest for "the realization of justice according to law." He offered impassioned testimony that "the form of justice will be without content till we fill it with the ardor of life." Not long after that, vigorous voices asserted that "the human rights part of the Constitution" had been excessively subordinated in order "to preserve the property rights part of same."[37]

After the cumulative impact of the anticommunist Palmer raids, cavalier disregard for civil liberties during the 1920s, judicial mishandling of the notorious Sacco-Vanzetti case, and the exposé of police abuses by the Wickersham Commission in 1931, some Americans concluded that the "contemporary attack on liberty" had to be stopped, that miscarriages of justice were occurring pervasively, and that "the nature of American liberty and justice" had become a sham.[38]

These were not altruistic Don Quixotes tilting at windmills. Throughout the 1920s a variety of conservative writers really did mount a sustained attack upon democracy, and insisted that uncontrolled democracy would utterly ruin American civilization. In 1920, for instance, Walter Lippmann urged his readers to recognize that the viability of liberty depended heavily upon public opinion. By 1928, worried about the prospects for order and authority, Lipp-

---

37. Hand, "The Speech of Justice" (1916) in Irving Dilliard, ed., *The Spirit of Liberty: Papers and Addresses of Learned Hand* (3rd ed.: Chicago, 1960), 14–15; Samuel Eliot Morison to Albert J. Beveridge, August 20, 1920, Beveridge Papers, box 222, Library of Congress, Manuscript Division, Washington, D.C.; Benjamin N. Cardozo, *The Nature of the Judicial Process* (New Haven, 1921), 66, 74, 120, 134, 137, 140, 149–50.

38. See Leon Whipple, *The Story of Civil Liberty in the United States* (New York, 1927), a serious book sponsored by the American Civil Liberties Union that reached a broad audience by means of a fifty-cent mass-market edition; James Truslow Adams to Mark DeWolfe Howe, November 16, 1929, Adams Papers, box 11, Butler Library, Columbia University, New York; Ernest Sutherland Bates, *This Land of Liberty* (New York, 1930), 5–6, 8. The story is told that Justice Oliver Wendell Holmes was once saying goodbye to Judge Learned Hand of the New York Court of Appeals. "Do justice!" said Hand. "That is not my job," Holmes replied. "My job is to play the game according to the rules."

mann announced: "It may well be that to limit the power of ma-
jorities, to dispute their moral authority, to deflect their impact,
to dissolve their force, is now the most important task of those
who care for liberty."[39]

In 1924, when James M. Beck (Solicitor General of the United
States) published a substantial volume on *The Constitution of the
United States: Yesterday, Today—and Tomorrow,* Calvin Coolidge
obliged him with a presidential foreword. Two more traditional
men, in terms of political philosophy, would be difficult to imag-
ine. Yet between them they turned "liberty and justice" into a cliché.
Coolidge declared that our government of law "signifies justice and
liberty." Beck asserted that "the great purpose of the Constitution
is to assert these eternal verities of liberty and justice." A few pages
later, still in his introduction, Beck assured readers that the Constitution remained "a noble and serviceable temple of Liberty and
Justice."[40] A slogan had come of age; and for the moment at least,
in a bipartisan way. In the eyes of conservatives, liberty and justice
had not supplanted liberty and order or liberty and property. It
had been hitched on to form a kind of holy political trinity.

In 1922, for example, newly appointed Chief Justice Taft published the Cutler Lecture that he had presented at the University
of Rochester a year before, entitled *Liberty Under Law.* In Taft's
case it seems fair to assert that the word *Under* really did have connotations of subordination. He pleaded for liberty and authority
in addition to the other eternal verities; he commented that "to
be useful, democracy and liberty must be regulated"; and he concluded that "liberty, abiding for each person, is impossible unless
it be ordered liberty."[41]

39. Compare Lippmann, *Liberty and the News* (New York, 1920), 96–97, with Lippmann, *American Inquisitors* (New York, 1928), 111; and see Ronald Steel, *Walter Lippmann
and the American Century* (New York, 1980), 171–72, 219, 234.

40. Beck, *The Constitution of the United States: Yesterday, Today—and Tomorrow?* (New
York, 1924), vi, ix, xi.

41. Taft, *Liberty Under Law: An Interpretation of the Principles of Our Constitutional
Government* (New Haven, 1922), esp. 47–48, 51.

Three years later, when Charles Evans Hughes gave his presidential address to the American Bar Association, his tone remained close to Taft's. It worried Hughes that some Americans still might equate democracy with liberty, and thereby fail to realize that democracy actually endangered liberty. To use his own words: "Democracy has its own capacity for tyranny. Some of the most menacing encroachments upon liberty invoke the democratic principle and assert the right of the majority to rule." What did Hughes value above all? For what did he plead most urgently? He repeated it four times — "a well-ordered freedom" — and he ended with an exaltation to "the authority of law as the servant of liberty wisely conceived." Liberty and justice had little appeal for Hughes in 1925.[42]

In 1932, when architect Cass Gilbert sent Elihu Root photographs of the new Supreme Court building, that eminent corporation lawyer and former Secretary of War and Republican Senator responded with lavish praise, with a lament that poor Taft had gone to his eternal home, and with hosannas for the Supreme Court's role in "the preservation of liberty and order."[43]

Once the New Deal got under way in 1933–34, conservatives who clung to liberty as their banner did so more in the name of liberty and property than liberty and order. They insisted that government had an obligation to protect private property and individual liberty to the fullest, while doing less centralizing and regulating. Ogden L. Mills, who had served as Herbert Hoover's Secretary of the Treasury, equated liberty with free enterprise, and com-

---

42. Hughes, "Liberty and Law," *Report of the 48th Annual Meeting of the American Bar Association* (Baltimore, 1925), 185–89, 195, 199. See also Samuel Hendel, *Charles Evans Hughes and the Supreme Court* (New York, 1951), ch. 2, "The Reconciliation of Liberty and Authority."

43. Root to Gilbert, February 25, 1932, Cass Gilbert Papers, box 13, Library of Congress, Manuscript Division, Washington, D.C. See also the speech that David M. Matteson drafted for Senator John H. Overton of Louisiana in September 1937. "Ordered liberty was the watchword of Washington, Madison, Wilson, Morris, Franklin, King, Sherman . . . and all the others who in their convention at Philadelphia 150 years ago framed our Constitution. . . ." Matteson Papers, box 1, National Archives (Record Group 200), Washington, D.C.

plained in 1935 that "we have sacrificed Constitutional Liberty to the god of planning." On May 4, 1935, Colonel Robert R. Mc-Cormick, publisher and editor of the *Chicago Tribune*, addressed a mass meeting of the Sentinels of the Republic (an archconservative organization) at Faneuil Hall in Boston. "Liberty is necessary to progress and civilization," he declared. "Liberty to unite, liberty to organize invention into production, liberty to exercise the virtues of industry and thrift, that production may multiply and its fruits be made available to all."[44]

Supporters of the New Deal regarded rhetoric of that sort as so much cant. An editorial in *The Nation* blasted the American Liberty League for its selfish traditionalism:

> We are, of course, under no illusion as to what these eminent men have in mind when they use the word "liberty." Their language is clear. They promise in their preliminary statement, first, to uphold the Constitution of the United States. Second, they will teach the necessity of respect for the rights of persons *and property*, "as fundamental to any successful form of government." . . . Despite the passing slight reference to the "rights of persons," this is an organization to secure to capitalism the power to live and do business as heretofore. Its conception of liberty is the right to maintain the old, discredited order, the liberty to continue an inequitable division of the products of labor, the liberty of some men through special privilege and government favoritism, or by the absence of government control, to build up large fortunes.[45]

Franklin D. Roosevelt, meanwhile, moved slowly but steadily away from the traditional notions of liberty that he had articulated as recently as 1932. He did so at first by speaking with scorn of the dire warnings offered by his critics. In a message to Congress on June 8, 1934, for example, Roosevelt said: "It is true that there

---

44. Mills, "Constitutional Liberty," *Vital Speeches of the Day* 1 (May 6, 1935): 491–95; McCormick, "The Torch of Liberty," ibid., 524–26. See also Paul S. Whitcomb to Lyon G. Tyler, July 30, 1932, Tyler Papers, Swem Library, College of William and Mary, Williamsburg, Virginia; Worthington C. Ford to James Truslow Adams, June 3, 1936, James Truslow Adams Papers, Butler Library, Columbia University, New York.

45. *The Nation* 139 (September 5, 1934): 257.

are a few among us who would still go back. . . . They loudly assert that individual liberty is being restricted by Government, but when they are asked what individual liberties they have lost, they are put to it to answer." In his second Fireside Chat of 1934, broadcast on September 30, Roosevelt explained that he opposed "a return to that definition of liberty under which for many years a free people were being gradually regimented into the service of the privileged few. I prefer and I am sure you prefer that broad definition of liberty under which we are moving forward to greater freedom, to greater security for the average man than he has ever known before in the history of America." On September 17, 1937, when FDR presented his highly political Constitution Day address to millions of radio listeners, he added his prestige to those who had already made the link between liberty and justice a maxim of New Deal objectives and social thought.[46]

For moderate, middle-of-the-road Americans, 1936 seems to have been a pivotal year in reassessing old and new notions of liberty. As both Francis W. Coker (president of the American Political Science Association in 1936) and George Soule explained, Americans were confronting a fundamental "conflict of ideas—the conflict between necessity for change and loyalty to American tradition." Soule, an advocate of social and economic planning, regarded "liberty for business enterprise" and liberty with justice for ordinary wage earners as absolutely irreconcilable. He concluded that "the two sorts of liberty are incompatible" and tried to contemplate whether socialism could have adverse implications for liberty. Coker observed that opponents of the New Deal did not seem to be concerned about liberty in general, only about economic liberty, and concluded with a judicious vision of older views being

46. Roosevelt, "Message to the Congress Reviewing the Broad Objectives and Accomplishments of the Administration," June 8, 1934, in Rosenman, ed., *Public Papers and Addresses of Franklin D. Roosevelt*, 3:292; Roosevelt, "First Fireside Chat," June 28, 1934, ibid., 314; Roosevelt, "Second Fireside Chat," September 30, 1934, ibid., 422. See also Michael E. Parrish, *Felix Frankfurter and His Times: The Reform Years* (New York, 1982), 272 and 321 n. 90.

adapted to newer needs: "There are respectable American traditions for Capitalists, for Socialists, for Reformers, and, finally, for genuine individualists—those who (following Jefferson) desire to see private property maintained along with guarantees for some sort of equality in the operation of the system."[47]

By the middle and later 1930s it seemed clear to a majority of Americans that "liberty and property" as well as "ordered liberty" were selfish slogans that best served the ideological goals of special interest groups. That recognition made it possible—even necessary—for many leaders to replace these slogans with either "liberty and justice" or else with a reformulation of liberty in terms of economic need.[48] In 1939, for example, a liberal Congressman from San Antonio, Maury Maverick, published a popular little book of basic American documents introduced by his own analysis of their implications for contemporary society. Entitled *In Blood and Ink: The Life and Documents of American Democracy*, the book presented on its cover a statement of Maverick's credo: "Democracy, to me, is liberty *plus* economic security. To put it in plain language, we Americans want to talk, pray, think as we please—and eat regular. I say this because there is a lot of nonsense in talk about liberty. You cannot fill the baby's bottle with liberty."

Growing awareness of the rise of fascist and communist dictatorships in Europe gave this reassessment greater urgency. For a decade following the mid-1920s, however, the powerful sway of American isolationism was such that only occasional expressions of concern appeared. *The Nation* remarked in an editorial that "unless we can find through democracy a way to efficiency, justice, and liberty,

47. Coker, "American Traditions Concerning Property and Liberty," *American Political Science Review* 30 (February 1936): 1–23, esp. 22; Soule, *The Future of Liberty* (New York, 1936), 164–65.

48. See *New York Times*, June 22, 1938, p. 5; ibid., April 19, 1939, p. 25; and *De Jonge v. Oregon*, 299 U.S. 353 (1937).

we shall get dictatorship—and we shall deserve it." And Lincoln Steffens declared in 1931 that the communists (presumably meaning the U.S.S.R.) do not envy "our justice, liberty and democracy."[49] But such comments were not commonplace before the mid-1930s.

Thereafter it became much less acceptable to speak or write about the need to "regulate" democracy. Developments in Europe during the later 1930s caused large numbers of Americans to feel that perhaps the United States took its heritage of liberty too much for granted. As a result, organizational efforts were undertaken to re-educate the citizenry about the Bill of Rights, about the sacrifices that had been made in the struggle to create free institutions, and about "the spiritual implications of liberty." For the first time in many, many years, liberty tended to be discussed in terms of external threats rather than in terms of internal structures of governmental authority and domestic disorder and instability.

In June 1938 a nonpartisan organization known as National rededication was formed in New York City in order to promote a campaign on behalf of liberty and democracy. A statement issued by the sponsors declared that "liberty has been destroyed in many of the leading nations." The national advisory committee included James Truslow Adams, John W. Davis, Dorothy Canfield Fisher, Herbert Hoover, Alfred M. Landon, Mrs. Arthur Hays Sulzberger, Norman Thomas, William Allen White, Mary E. Woolley, and Owen D. Young. Hermann Hagedorn, a disciple of Theodore Roosevelt, served as acting director and explained that "we are not interested in criticizing anybody or attacking anybody. Our purpose is to state the case for liberty and democracy as expressed in the Declaration of Independence and guaranteed by the Constitution of the United States." The campaign would be carried on primarily through churches, schools, the press, radio, and motion pictures.[50]

49. "The Day of the Dictator," *The Nation* 117 (September 26, 1923): 312; *The Autobiography of Lincoln Steffens* (New York, 1931), 837. See also Roosevelt, "Address on Constitution Day," September 17, 1937, in Rosenman, ed., *Public Papers and Addresses of Franklin D. Roosevelt*, 6:359–60.

50. *New York Times*, June 8, 1938, p. 3; ibid., June 9, 1938, p. 22, editorial entitled

By 1941 a broad array of organizations and individuals, despite their ideological diversity, shared a new enthusiasm for the Bill of Rights and a common vocabulary to be used when their objectives required succinct articulation. In Henry Luce's influential statement called "The American Century" (1941) he described America as "the powerhouse of the ideals of Freedom and Justice." Early that year Helen Keller had made the same linkage in letters to other American patriots.[51]

Renewed attention to the Bill of Rights made those lapidary inscriptions on the new Supreme Court building (opened in October 1935) even more meaningful: "Equal Justice Under Law" and "Justice the Guardian of Liberty."

Late in 1941, when the nation observed the sesquicentennial of ratification of the Bill of Rights, *The New York Times* published a lengthy editorial. Its emotional core was a plea that the United States dedicate itself "to save the spirit of the Bill of Rights and, with God's help, to establish it as the rule of life on earth. To peoples crushed and bleeding under the totalitarian juggernaut our action says: 'Take heart! Have hope! Liberty and justice have not perished.'"[52] "Liberty and justice" seems rather an apt epigram with which to summarize the meaning of the Bill of Rights. In so far as those amendments have been far more visible in public life since 1940 than before then, it is both appropriate as well as understandable that the slogan itself would enjoy broader usage.

Prominent jurists did much to make it so. In 1940, for example, Harlan Fiske Stone's resounding dissent on behalf of two children (Jehovah's Witnesses) who refused on religious grounds to salute

---

"Rededicating America"; Hermann Hagedorn to James Truslow Adams, May 31 and June 23, 1938, Adams Papers, Butler Library, Columbia University, New York.

51. Luce is quoted by Daniel Bell, "The End of American Exceptionalism," in Nathan Glazer and Irving Kristol, eds., *The American Commonwealth, 1976* (New York, 1976), 203; Helen Keller to James Truslow Adams, January 3, 1941, Adams Papers, Butler Library, Columbia University, New York. See also *The Bill of Rights Review: A Quarterly* 1 (Summer 1940): 3.

52. *New York Times*, December 15, 1941, p. 18.

the flag declared that for the Supreme Court to defer to Pennsylvania state law would be "no less than the surrender of the constitutional protection of the liberty of small minorities to the popular will." Stone's dissent, which swiftly became the view dominant by 1943, also insisted that the

> Constitution expresses more than the conviction of the people that democratic processes must be preserved at all costs. It is also an expression of faith and a command that freedom of mind and spirit must be preserved, which government must obey, if it is to adhere to that justice and moderation without which no free government can exist.[53]

From the later 1920s until 1940, when he wrote the Court's opinion in the *Gobitis* case (provoking Stone's dissent quoted above), Felix Frankfurter had been explicitly preoccupied with the problem of reconciling liberty and authority. By 1943 his orientation began to shift somewhat, and he supported his opinions with an altered set of fundamental concerns: "When we are dealing with the Constitution of the United States, and more particularly with the great safeguards of the Bill of Rights, we are dealing with principles of liberty and justice 'so rooted in the traditions and conscience of our people as to be ranked as fundamental'—something without which 'a fair and enlightened system of justice would be impossible.'"[54]

In a talk called "Liberty" given at Yale in 1941, Learned Hand proclaimed that "the dawn of social justice has [now] broken into bright unclouded day."[55] Ugly episodes that occurred during and after World War II cause Hand's optimism to sound excessively pollyanna-ish. Nevertheless, abundant evidence from the 1940s also

---

53. *Minersville School District et al. v. Gobitis*, 310 U.S. 586 (1940), the quotations at 606, 607. For historical context, see Herbert Wechsler, "Mr. Justice Stone and the Constitution," in Wechsler, *Principles, Politics, and Fundamental Law: Selected Essays* (Cambridge, MA, 1961), 126–37.

54. Parrish, *Frankfurter and His Times: The Reform Years*, 168; *Minersville School District et al. v. Gobitis*, 310 U.S. 586 (1940), at 591; *Bridges v. California*, 314 U.S. 252 (1941), at 279, 284; *West Virginia State Board of Education v. Barnette*, 319 U.S. 624 (1943), at 652.

55. Hand, "Liberty" (1941) in Dilliard, ed., *The Spirit of Liberty*, 147.

makes it apparent that aroused sensitivity to liberty and justice as a social imperative was spreading.[56] It was suitably symbolic that when Judge Hand delivered his second "I Am an American Day" address in Central Park, New York, on May 20, 1945, he closed by inviting the audience to join in the (by then) official pledge of allegiance. There was many a moist eye, and many throats with unswallowed lumps, as the last six words were recited: "with liberty and justice for all."[57]

From the later 1940s until the mid-1960s, years commonly recognized as a time of Cold War tension between the United States and the Soviet Union, anxieties about domestic as well as international security may have initially constrained this thrust toward expanded liberty; but in the long run the stresses of that period served as a powerful stimulus to regain the momentum that had been achieved in the decade following 1938. Herman Belz's analysis of American constitutionalism during the Cold War era itself, however, is fundamentally correct: "Liberty was more often defined in negative terms—as freedom from rather than freedom to—and with good reason in view of the ubiquitous loyalty programs inspired by anti-communism."[58]

It cannot be denied that such legislation as the Internal Security Act of 1950, the Communist Control Act of 1954, and an interminable series of congressional investigations, collectively had

56. Dixon Ryan Fox, "Free Speech in Times of Strain," unpublished address given at Union College, June 8, 1940, Fox Papers, Schaffer Library, Union College, Schenectady, New York; a letter to *The New York Times*, written by Erwin Griswold and Benjamin Cohen in 1942, quoted in Anthony Lewis, *Gideon's Trumpet* (New York, 1964), 138; Charles A. Beard, *The Republic: Conversations on Fundamentals* (New York, 1943), 125, 128.

57. Hand, "A Pledge of Allegiance" (1945) in Dilliard, ed., *The Spirit of Liberty*, 192–94.

58. Stanley I. Kutler, *The American Inquisition: Justice and Injustice in the Cold War* (New York, 1982); Belz, "Changing Conceptions of Constitutionalism in the Era of World War II and the Cold War," *Journal of American History* 59 (December 1972): 657.

the effect of constraining civil liberties. For many Americans, security may very well have become a higher priority than either liberty or justice.[59] Courageous individuals responded, however, and they utilized the media effectively. "What sets me apart from Senator McCarthy," news broadcaster Edward R. Murrow explained on one of his CBS programs, "is my devotion to the principles upon which this nation rests—justice, freedom and fairness." When "Omnibus" presented a three-part series on the Constitution during the spring of 1956, Joseph N. Welch (Senator McCarthy's feisty antagonist earlier in the decade) served successfully as narrator. The third installment in that series, an exploration of constitutional issues from 1864 until 1942, was entitled "With Liberty and Justice for All," and it stressed the importance of protecting civil liberties. Various local stations reinforced this emphasis. In 1959, for example, the educational staff at WJAR–TV in Providence, Rhode Island, organized a series of programs called "The American Tradition," and devoted one installment to "The American Tradition of Law and Justice."[60]

Although liberals may have been more likely than conservatives to answer situations and events with varied applications of "liberty and justice," it is striking that throughout the 1950s and 60s no single segment of the ideological spectrum monopolized the phrase. Patriotic American tourists who visited Colonial Williamsburg were likely to use it when they wrote letters of appreciation to John D. Rockefeller, Jr. Traditional academic philosophers relied upon it in explaining the nature of American democracy. Congressmen used it in defending the necessity for an independent ju-

59. See Alfred H. Kelly, ed., *Foundations of Freedom in the American Constitution* (New York, 1958), esp. the essays by Kelly, "Where Constitutional Liberty Came From," 47–49; Jack W. Peltason, "Constitutional Liberty and the Communist Problem," 113–39; Robert K. Carr, "Constitutional Liberty and Congressional Investigations," 140–92; and Alan F. Westin, "Constitutional Liberty and Loyalty Programs," 193–250.

60. Joseph Wershba, "Murrow vs. McCarthy: See It Now," *The New York Times Magazine*, March 4, 1979, p. 31; Joseph N. Welch with Richard Hofstadter, *The Constitution* (Boston, 1956), esp. Part Three and p. 89; Betty Adams to Mark Howe, Jr., March 4, 1959, Howe Papers, box 6, fol. 11, Harvard Law School Library, Cambridge, Massachusetts.

diciary that would be free from politically motivated threats of impeachment.[61]

The Fund for the Republic, established during the 1950s as an antidote to the national obsession with international conspiracy and internal subversion, sponsored an American Traditions contest that made "freedom with justice" its theme. It also presented annual awards to the best television programs dealing with freedom and justice. The U.S. Congress, which had not passed any civil rights legislation since 1875, finally did so in 1957, and in the process revealed a degree of responsiveness to the concern for liberty and justice that had been growing for nearly two decades. An editorial that appeared in *Life* – a magazine which reflected the nation's moderately conservative mood – conceded that the segregation cases that came before the Supreme Court in 1954–55 "offered an opportunity to restate some fundamental principles of liberty and justice. . . ."[62]

Major opinions promulgated by justices of the high court, along with essays and addresses that they presented off the bench, invoked that phrase frequently during the post-war era. Frank Murphy felt moved to do so in 1946 when dissenting in an appeal that anticipated the celebrated case of *Gideon v. Wainwright* (1963). Hugo Black's famous dissent in *Adamson v. California* (1947), arguing that the Bill of Rights should apply in state as well as Federal courts, stressed the absolute need for "fundamental liberty and justice." Harold H. Burton called attention to the motto "Justice is the Guardian of Liberty" in an essay that he published in 1951.[63]

---

61. See Louise Morris Mills to John D. Rockefeller, Jr., December 12, 1950, Rockefeller Papers, Series II (Cultural), 2E, box 177, Rockefeller Archive Center, Pocantico Hills, North Tarrytown, New York; George H. Sabine, "The Two Democratic Traditions," *The Philosophical Review* 61 (October 1952): 470; *The Autobiography of William O. Douglas: The Court Years, 1939–1975* (New York, 1980), 87, 88.

62. The Fund for the Republic Papers, an underutilized treasure-trove, are located in the Seeley G. Mudd Manuscript Library at Princeton University, Princeton, New Jersey; Will Maslow and Joseph B. Robison, "Civil Rights Legislation and the Fight for Equality, 1862–1952," *University of Chicago Law Review* 20 (Spring 1953): 363–413; "The Trouble with the Warren Court," *Life Magazine* 44 (June 16, 1958): 35.

63. *Carter v. Illinois*, 329 U.S. 173 (1946), at 183; *Adamson v. California*, 332 U.S. 46

When Earl Warren agreed to write an essay on law for a lay audience, he chose as his theme "the ideal of liberty and justice under law," and he expressed earnest hope for an improvement in "the administration of justice and strengthening liberty under law."[64] William O. Douglas, who shared Warren's concern, recounted in his autobiography an interview at the White House with Lyndon B. Johnson in 1967. Justice Tom Clark had recently died, and Johnson wanted to discuss possible nominees with Douglas.

> He mentioned names and I commented on them. Regarding one, I said, "He will be very conservative on economic matters, and occasionally for liberty and justice on other matters." "Liberty and justice," he said, "that's all you apparently think of. And when you pass over the last hill, I suppose you will be shouting 'Liberty and justice!'"[65]

It should not be assumed, however, that the justices completely abandoned all previous formulations. In 1954, when Robert H. Jackson prepared his Godkin Lectures for presentation at Harvard, he ascribed to the founders an eighteenth-century world-view in which the "truths of natural law . . . stood as the ultimate sanction of liberty and justice, equality and toleration." In his third lecture, however, where he discussed the Court as a political institution, Jackson stressed a concern that many of his contemporaries still shared: "In a society in which rapid changes tend to upset all equilibrium, the Court, without exceeding its own limited powers, must strive to maintain the great system of balances upon which our free government is based." Among these he included the need for parity "between authority, be it state or national, and the liberty of the citizen. . . ."[66]

A few years earlier, in a very complicated ruling that required

(1947), at 69 and 89; Burton, "'Justice the Guardian of Liberty': John Marshall at the Trial of Aaron Burr," *American Bar Association Journal* 37 (October 1951): 735–38.

64. Warren, "The Law and the Future," *Fortune* 52 (November 1955): 224, 229, 230.

65. Douglas, *The Court Years, 1939–1975*, 329.

66. Jackson, *The Supreme Court in the American System of Government* (Cambridge, MA, 1955), 3, 61.

officers of labor unions to forswear membership in the Communist Party, Justice Jackson had written an opinion that dissented in part from the majority view but also concurred in part, an ambivalent response that was highly unusual at the time though not without precedent. (It has become commonplace on the Court during the past generation.) After conceding that a democracy must protect freedom of belief, Jackson insisted that the Communist Party was unlike other political parties in the United States because it was dominated by a foreign government. He then wrote a sentence that clearly placed him in the Holmes-Frankfurter tradition of jurists who believed that situations arise in which justice might have to suffer because of limitations in the prevailing law or tradition of jurisprudence: "The task of this Court to maintain a balance between liberty and authority is never done, because new conditions today upset the equilibriums of yesterday."[67]

Nevertheless, the notion of liberty and justice not only gained popularity, it attained such ubiquitous usage that by the 1960s it had nearly become a hackneyed cliché, casually employed by spokesmen for all segments of society. In 1963 a sign appeared in the Jackson, Mississippi, office of the Student Nonviolent Coordinating Committee:

> There is a place in Mississippi called Liberty
> There is a department in Washington called Justice.

A year later, when Barry Goldwater accepted the Republican nomination for President, he taunted moderates with these memorable

---

67. *American Communications Association, C.I.O., et al. v. Douds, Regional Director of the National Labor Relations Board*, 339 U.S. 382 (1950), at 445. See the opening sentence of Frankfurter's opinion for the Court in *Minersville School District et al. v. Gobitis*, 310 U.S. 586 (1940), at 591. "A grave responsibility confronts this Court whenever in course of litigation it must reconcile the conflicting claims of liberty and authority. But when the liberty invoked is liberty of conscience, and the authority is authority to safeguard the nation's fellowship, judicial conscience is put to its severest test." When Charles A. Beard spoke at the University of Virginia in 1943, he too highlighted the problem of achieving equilibrium between liberty and authority. See Ellen Nore, *Charles A. Beard: An Intellectual Biography* (Carbondale, 1983), 193.

lines: "Extremism in defense of liberty is no vice. And . . . moderation in pursuit of justice is no virtue."[68]

One other ramification of liberty and justice requires attention. By the mid-1960s that phrase struck such a compelling note that Justice Arthur Goldberg used it in his controversial concurring opinion to support the decision in *Griswold v. Connecticut*, which legalized the sale of contraceptive devices. The key concept in the resolution of that case was "the right to privacy," a right that is not explicitly provided for in the Constitution, but one that caused some Americans to cultivate a logical linkage between liberty and privacy.[69]

Interestingly enough, in cases prior to *Griswold*, where the Supreme Court had upheld state prohibitions of contraceptive sales, the ideal of liberty had been carefully explored in terms of its potential relevance. In 1961, for example, John Marshall Harlan dissented when the Court allowed Connecticut's statute to stand. His language turned out to be prescient.

> The full scope of the liberty guaranteed by the Due Process Clause cannot be found in or limited by the precise terms of the specific guarantees elsewhere provided in the Constitution. This "liberty" is not a series of isolated points pricked out in terms of the taking of property. . . . It is a rational continuum which, broadly speaking, includes a freedom from all substantial arbitrary impositions and purposeless restraints. . . .[70]

The Court's 1973 decision, *Roe v. Wade*, which legalized abortion during the first trimester of pregnancy, conceded that the right to

---

68. Quoted in Allen J. Matusow, *The Unraveling of America: A History of Liberalism in the 1960s* (New York, 1984), 82, 137. An organization called The Los Angeles Committee for the Protection of the Foreign Born took as its motto "With Liberty & Justice for All." See *Constitutional Protection for the Foreign Born*, 12th Annual Conference Journal (Los Angeles, 1962).

69. *Griswold v. Connecticut*, 381 U.S. 478 (1965), at 493, where Goldberg quoted from *Powell v. Alabama*, 287 U.S. 45 (1932 [the first Scottsboro Case]), at 67. See also Paul L. Murphy, *The Constitution in Crisis Times, 1918–1969* (New York, 1972), 402; and Clinton Rossiter, "The Pattern of Liberty," in Milton R. Konvitz and Clinton Rossiter, eds., *Aspects of Liberty: Essays Presented to Robert E. Cushman* (Ithaca, 1958), 17.

70. *Poe et al. v. Ullman, State's Attorney*, 367 U.S. 497 (1961), at 543.

privacy is not absolute, yet grounded the right of privacy in such matters in "the concept of liberty guaranteed by the first section of the Fourteenth Amendment." Constitutional scholars have quarreled bitterly over the relevance (and metaphysical meaning) of liberty and justice as applied to *Roe v. Wade.*[71] All we can say with assurance at this point is that ever since 1965 the connection between liberty and privacy has acquired a legitimacy and a resonance that it did not previously enjoy. Pertinent issues include not merely the purchase of contraceptives and the "right" to have an abortion, but the right to show pornographic films within one's own home. In 1969 a unanimous Court held that the

> right to receive information and ideas, regardless of their social worth . . . is fundamental to our free society. . . . Also fundamental is the right to be free, except in very limited circumstances, from unwanted governmental intrusions into one's privacy. . . . We think that mere categorization of these films as "obscene" is insufficient justification for such a drastic invasion of personal liberties guaranteed by the First and Fourteenth Amendments.

The Court concluded with a strong appeal to "traditional notions of individual liberty," and insisted that a person's right to read or view whatever he pleases is "fundamental to our scheme of individual liberty."[72] Individual liberty joined with personal privacy may not yet enjoy an unchallenged place in the pantheon of American freedoms; but after twenty years of supportive decisions, its niche is looking more and more secure.

There is one other connection between liberty and a potentially complementary quality that has not yet been mentioned. Its ab-

71. *Roe et al. v. Wade,* 410 U.S. 113 (1973), 116–71 for the opinions in full. See Eva R. Rubin, *Abortion, Politics, and the Courts: Roe v. Wade and Its Aftermath* (Westport, CT, 1982); and "Of Roe v. Wade and the Line between Justice and Liberty," a letter to the editor from Professor Leonard Binder, *New York Times,* February 18, 1983, p. A30.

72. *Stanley v. Georgia,* 394 U.S. 557 (1969), esp. at 564, 565, 568.

sence is simultaneously significant, regrettable, and yet defensible on historical grounds. I have in mind liberty and equality, of course, a match that has occasionally but not commonly been made in the United States and that has just as frequently been rejected (though neither often nor very openly during the past half-century), and a relationship that until fairly recently remained both ambiguous and problematic.

In attempting to understand why the coupling of liberty and equality has been complicated in the United States, it should be noticed, first of all, that unlike all of the other linkages, this one has neither deep historical roots nor particularly strong parallels (until well into the twentieth century) in Great Britain. Although we do find in "Cato's Letters" (for July 1, 1721) the assertion that "Liberty can never subsist without Equality," that was not a theme that the Real Whigs elaborated in any sustained way. More familiar —and more nearly characteristic, perhaps—was Coleridge's mockery during the 1790s of those radical reformers whose motto was "Liberty and Equality."[73]

That slogan, and the ideological impulse behind it, has a more sporadic and pejorative history in Great Britain than in the United States. In 1875 the young Frederic William Maitland, destined to become the master of English legal history, attempted a prize essay on the problematic subject "Liberty and Equality." The essay was not very good and subsequently became an embarrassment to him. George Orwell—to select a twentieth-century figure—regarded the United States as the land of liberty but decidedly *not* a land of equality.[74]

73. Jacobson, ed., *English Libertarian Heritage*, 91–92; Dickinson, *Liberty and Property*, 258. For Harold J. Laski's view that liberty and equality are complementary (revisionist against Lord Acton's belief to the contrary), see Laski, *Liberty in the Modern State* (London, 1930), 16–19. In a letter to John C. H. Wu, June 21, 1928, Oliver Wendell Holmes referred to Laski's "passion for Equality, with which I have no sympathy at all." See Max Lerner, ed., *The Mind and Faith of Justice Holmes* (Boston, 1943), 435.

74. C. H. S. Fifoot, *Frederic William Maitland: A Life* (Cambridge, MA, 1971), 46–48; Orwell, "Mark Twain—The Licensed Jester" (1943), in Sonia Orwell and Ian Angus, eds., *The Collected Essays, Journalism and Letters of George Orwell* (London, 1968), 2:325–29.

We achieve some illumination if we recall that ever since the French Revolution of 1789, Liberty and Equality has been regarded as a concept especially meaningful to the French. By the mid-1790s, in fact, it had acquired negative connotations in the United States for those enamoured of liberty and order. An American attack on the French Revolution as political perversion referred to Brissot de Warville's ideas with contempt: "If he could even convince us of the efficacity of his remedy (Liberty and Equality) we should certainly reject it as ten thousand times worse than the disease."[75] Mark Howe, the distinguished constitutional and legal historian, observed that the concept of equality did not even appear in American constitutional law until adoption of the Fourteenth Amendment by the states in 1868, and he added that Americans showed scant interest in enforcing the spirit of liberty and equality until well after World War II.[76]

It would be incorrect to assume, however, that "liberty and equality" has been totally absent from public discourse in the United States. During the later 1790s, Jeffersonians might on occasion erect a liberty pole bearing the motto "Liberty and Equality." When Edward Everett delivered a Fourth of July oration in 1828 he lauded "the day when, for the first time in the world, a numerous people was ushered into the family of nations, organized on the principle of the political equality of all the citizens."[77] Andrew Jackson hoped that his fellow citizens would find in his farewell address "an ear-

---

See also the fierce attack by James Fitzjames Stephen, *Liberty, Equality, Fraternity* (London, 1873), directed particularly at John Stuart Mill's *On Liberty* (London, 1859).

75. Anon., in *The American Monthly Review; or Literary Journal* 1 (January 1795): 19; David Tappan, *Christian Thankfulness Explained and Enforced. A Sermon Delivered at Charlestown . . . February 19, 1795 . . .* (Boston, 1795), 21–22; Nathan O. Hatch, *The Sacred Cause of Liberty: Republican Thought and the Millennium in Revolutionary New England* (New Haven, 1977), 123; and see the interview with William T. Coleman, Jr., in *The New York Times*, April 20, 1982, p. D21: "France taught us a lot about liberty and equality."

76. Howe, "Problems of Religious Liberty," in Carl J. Friedrich, ed., *Liberty* (Nomos, 4) (New York, 1962), 271. See also Roscoe Pound, "Liberty of Contract," *Yale Law Journal* 18 (May 1909): 484.

77. See Irving Brant, *Storm Over the Constitution* (Indianapolis, 1936), 216; Everett,

nest desire to perpetuate in this favored land the blessings of liberty and equal law." The opening sentence of Abraham Lincoln's Gettysburg Address, of course, identified this as a nation "conceived in Liberty, and dedicated to the proposition that all men are created equal."[78]

Despite a few rather curious claims to the contrary, however, the U.S. Supreme Court showed relatively little interest in liberty and equality during the first century and two-thirds of its existence. Much more characteristic are these words, spoken by Justice David J. Brewer in 1902 at a dinner given by the Bar of the Supreme Court (i.e., lawyers who had been admitted to practice before it) in honor of Justice John Marshall Harlan. At one point in his largely laudatory speech, Brewer offered a peculiar observation – peculiar only in view of the occasion:

> Brother Harlan made a mistake in holding that the Civil Rights Bill was constitutional. The Court said so; and in our governmental system the Supreme Court, on constitutional questions, is infallible, though, as every one knows, no one of its members ever comes within sight or sound of infallibility. But it was a mistake on the side of equal rights, and no act done or word said in behalf of liberty and equality ever fails to touch humanity with inspiring, prophetic thrill.

A strange and sardonic mishmash, at first glance, until we recognize the candor of Brewer's message. The rhetoric of liberty and equality may be highly inspirational; but the doctrine itself is socially unrealistic and lacks any legal foundation. In its mixed and modified form, however, the rhetoric must have retained an irresistible quality; for in the very next paragraph Brewer praised "those eternal principles of justice, liberty, and equality without which

---

"The History of Liberty," an oration delivered at Charlestown, Massachusetts, July 4, 1828, in Everett, *Orations and Speeches on Various Occasions* (9th ed.: Boston, 1878), 1:151. See also Sean Wilentz, *Chants Democratic: New York City & the Rise of the American Working Class, 1788–1850* (New York, 1984), 207.

78. Richardson, ed., *Messages and Papers of the Presidents*, 3:293; Basler, ed., *Collected Works of Lincoln*, 7:19.

the fathers believed that no free republic could ever endure and prosper."[79]

American ambivalence about the concept of equality, as Perry Miller suggested in 1955, dates from Jacksonian days.[80] For approximately a century thereafter, Americans of very different ideological dispositions were far more concerned about the inevitability of friction than persuaded of the possible compatibility between liberty and equality. A conservative like Arthur Twining Hadley, the President of Yale, interpreted liberty as life without governmental intervention. Because men were naturally unequal, to alter their relationship would necessitate an active role for government. Hence, in Hadley's view, liberty and equality were natural enemies.[81] A great many Americans, social elite and intelligentsia alike, shared that attitude during the first third of the twentieth century.

By the mid-1930s a change had begun to appear. Not many writers addressed themselves to the question; but those who did generally agreed that a fundamental tension existed between liberty and equality. One author, a professor of education and the head of Columbia Teachers' College, believed that the founders of the nation had really wanted both, though they may have been unrealistic. The ideal solution would require a program of com-

79. See Mark DeWolfe Howe, ed., *James Bradley Thayer, Oliver Wendell Holmes, and Felix Frankfurter on John Marshall* (Chicago, 1967), 155; a lengthy extract from Brewer's address appears in Alan F. Westin, ed., *An Autobiography of the Supreme Court: Off-the-Bench Commentary by the Justices* (New York, 1963), 192–93.

80. Miller, "Equality in the American Setting," in John Crowell and Stanford J. Searl, Jr., eds., *The Responsibility of Mind in a Civilization of Machines: Essays by Perry Miller* (Amherst, MA, 1979), 156–57. See also Logan, *Liberty in the Modern World*, in 1928: "Liberty must in fact often become the bulwark and guarantor of inequality, of the opportunity of every man to cultivate his own peculiar talents and find his natural level in society" (9).

81. Hadley, *The Conflict Between Liberty and Equality* (Boston, 1925). For a latterday version of the same outlook, stimulated by the fear of racial integration, see Carter Pittman, *Equality v. Liberty: The Eternal Conflict* (Richmond, 1960), who praised the virtues of inequality and feared the onset of communism if equality between the races were forced.

promises. Americans would have to establish priorities and make trade-offs.[82]

Others with a more activist bent accepted the traditional view that liberty meant the absence of restraint upon individuals, and especially meant no government regulation. But they responded by subordinating or rejecting the customary sense of liberty as an unrealistic value under modern socio-economic conditions. George Soule spoke for large numbers of Americans—especially the generation just then coming of age—when he formulated the problem in these terms:

> You start with a nominally free society; then by the exercise of economic freedom some men acquire more power than others; a concentration of wealth grows. But economic power is political power. Equality vanishes. The forms of democracy, however, remain. The people continue to have faith in the government as their agency, and periodically try to use it to check the power that wealth has assumed, or try to redistribute the wealth itself. In so far as they succeed, the liberty of rich men is limited; if the masses are to have a lasting victory, the very kind of economic freedom out of which the successful competitors grew must be abolished. On the other hand, the power of wealth is likely to combat these efforts by taking the substance out of democracy.[83]

Soule was basically voicing the New Deal's social philosophy in rather generalized terms. Accepting renomination at Philadelphia on June 27, 1936, Franklin D. Roosevelt put it this way: "For too many of us the political equality we once had won was meaningless in the face of economic inequality. A small group had concentrated into their own hands an almost complete control over other people's property, other people's money, other people's labor—other people's lives. For too many of us life was no longer free; liberty no longer real; men could no longer follow the pursuit of happiness."[84]

82. William F. Russell, *Liberty vs. Equality* (New York, 1936).

83. Soule, *The Future of Liberty* (New York, 1936), 26.

84. Roosevelt, "We are Fighting to Save a Great and Precious Form of Government for Ourselves and the World," in Rosenman, ed., *Public Papers and Addresses of Franklin D. Roosevelt*, 5:233. Philippa Strum of Brooklyn College has contended that the New

By the middle and later 1930s, leaders of the professional movement known as legal realism began to supply answers to questions that had troubled them for almost a decade—such questions as: If law is simply what fallible courts and fallible men do, then what happens to the cherished ideal of law as the embodiment of justice? The threatening emergence of totalitarian states in Europe and East Asia made their concern all the more urgent. Americans who had been disillusioned with democracy ever since the collapse of Wilsonian idealism early in the 1920s felt compelled to reassess their political values. In 1940, for example, President Robert M. Hutchins of the University of Chicago presented a widely noticed convocation address there. He contended that democracy faced a grave crisis, and that it was the best form of government because it was the *only* form that could combine and supply three essential principles: law, equality, and justice.[85]

The lectures, books, and essays written during the 1940s by Edward S. Corwin, a distinguished professor of American constitutional history and jurisprudence at Princeton, enable us to trace in microcosm a broad and gradual shift. In 1941 Corwin juxtaposed liberty and equality as the word-symbols for two alternative modes of government:

> Under the democratic system there are two possible conceptions of what a government ought to be doing, provided neither is pressed to a logical extreme. One is that government ought to preserve an open field for talent and not disturb the rewards which free competition brings to individuals. The watchword of such a government will, of course, be Liberty. The other theory is that government ought to intervene for the purpose of correcting

Deal lacked any coherent view of the demands of liberty and equality, even though it dealt with issues that required a clear and consistent comprehension of those principles. Political needs rather than philosophical principles prevailed "and sowed, in turn, the seeds of our current confusions." John Agresto, ed., *Liberty and Equality under the Constitution* (Washington, D.C., 1983), 75–93.

85. Hutchins, "What Shall We Defend? We Are Losing Our Moral Principles," *Vital Speeches of the Day* 6 (July 1, 1940): 547. For historical context see Edward A. Purcell, Jr., *The Crisis of Democratic Theory: Scientific Naturalism & the Problem of Value* (Lexington, KY, 1973), chs. 7–9.

at least the more pronounced inequalities which are apt to result from the struggle for advantage among private groups and individuals. The watchword of such a government will be Equality.[86]

He believed that the achievement of social progress over an extended period of time required a kind of "alternation" between the two theories of government. Both were essential, and in roughly equal doses.

By 1948, however, Corwin acknowledged that in a broader perspective there was nothing incompatible about liberty and equality. In fact, elements in the American *cultural* tradition made possible their reconciliation.

> The term "liberty" has left behind the purely proprietarian connotations it inherited from the doctrine of vested rights, and in so doing it has taken on a distinctly equalitarian tinge. Nor is there anything exceptionable in this in itself. In the Ciceronian-Lockian conception of natural law, liberty and equality are not hostile, but friendly conceptions; and in the Declaration of Independence the same amicable relationship holds. . . . In the legalistic tradition, on which judicial review has operated in the past for the most part, "liberty" and "equality" are, on the other hand, apt to appear as opposed values, the former as the peculiar care of the courts, the latter the peculiar care of the legislature. It is easy to imagine in the light shed by current ideologies that the demands upon the legislative power, national and State, might so multiply in behalf of "the common man," whose century this is said to be, that the notion of Liberty against Government and its implement, judicial review, would be gradually but inexorably crowded to the wall.[87]

By 1950, when Corwin applied a kind of Darwinian mind-set to the evolution and survival of American political ideas, his thinking had shifted once again: in one sense with the times, but in another one might say that he actually anticipated major changes that would come very soon. "In the field of economic endeavor especially," he wrote, "'liberty,' which once stood at the head of the column of constitutional values, has been supplanted by 'equality.'

86. Corwin, *Constitutional Revolution, Ltd.* (Claremont, CA, 1941), 3–4.
87. Corwin, *Liberty Against Government*, 182. See also David M. Potter, *People of Plenty: Economic Abundance and the American Character* (Chicago, 1954), 92.

In terms of evolutionary theory, 'survival of the fittest' has given way to the right of all to survive in comfort so far as this can be contrived by governmental action."[88]

Within a decade, American political scientists, particularly disciples of Corwin, looked to other cultures for evidence that liberty and equality could be reconciled. Robert J. Harris, for instance, took comfort in the application of Stoic principles in ancient Rome: "Cicero began his discussion of liberty by proclaiming that liberty can abide only in those states in which the people have supreme power and in which liberty is equally enjoyed by all citizens. Liberty and equality were thus made indispensable complements to each other instead of possible opposites, which has been the fashion of some later writers."[89]

By 1980 the issue remained lively yet unresolved. Essays re-opened the debate over liberty versus equality by looking at it from fresh angles; and the National Humanities Center, located in North Carolina, sponsored a major conference devoted to the theme of Liberty and Equality under the Constitution. The critical issue has a familiar ring: "Is there a real tension, an irremedial tension, between the love of liberty and the demands of equality?"[90] I cannot say whether Cicero expected it to be resolved within his lifetime. I am not sanguine that it will even be clarified within my own.

In the last analysis two sorts of conclusions seem possible. The first is that while most of the antinomies we have considered may even-

88. Corwin, "The Impact of the Idea of Evolution on the American Political and Constitutional Tradition" (1950), in Richard Loss, ed., *Corwin on the Constitution* (Ithaca, 1981), 1:194.

89. Harris, *The Quest for Equality: The Constitution, Congress and the Supreme Court* (Baton Rouge, 1960), 5. The most important philosophical treatise written by an American since the 1960s, John Rawls's *A Theory of Justice* (Cambridge, MA, 1971), defined justice largely in terms of equality.

90. Herbert J. Gans, ed., *On the Making of Americans: Essays in Honor of David Riesman* (Philadelphia, 1979), esp. Richard Sennett, "What Tocqueville Feared," and Nathan

tually cease to be antinomies, they still do not cease to receive serious and sustained consideration. When the law school of Marquette University in Milwaukee, Wisconsin, celebrated its Golden Jubilee in 1959, it chose as its theme "The Rule of Law—Bulwark of Ordered Liberty." Justice Tom Clark, the principal speaker, posed this question: "What is 'liberty'?" and promptly conceded that although it is a "mighty word," it is also "an abstract one—having such meanings as one injects into it. Thus, its significance tends to change from person to person and from time to time." Clark then proceeded to cite only one among our several sets, liberty and equality, but he moved from there to a traditional notion of civil liberty that would have seemed commonplace in the Lockean climate of the mideighteenth century. A year later, in 1960, Henry Steele Commager warned that the ancient conundrum persisted: "the problem of the balance of order and liberty, the most ancient, the most recent, and in many ways the most difficult of all political problems."[91]

Other sets of dualisms, meanwhile, have turned out not to be mutually exclusive. Justice Hugo Black, for example, believed in liberty and order almost as fervently as he felt committed to liberty and justice. Recent writers of the neoconservative stripe, convinced that the free enterprise system is just, have sought to show that liberty (in the nineteenth-century sense) is entirely compatible with justice. Authors of this persuasion argue against government intervention and in favor of using the private sector in order to achieve social goals. They also seek to outline the agenda of moral values

Glazer, "Individualism and Equality in the United States," 105–26 and 127–42; Sidney Verba and Gary R. Orren, *Equality in America: The View from the Top* (Cambridge, MA, 1985), esp. 21–51; National Humanities Center *Newsletter* 2 (Fall 1980): 12–15. Political theorists who are partial to liberty but hostile to equality have an interesting and plausible interpretation of the founders' understanding of the relationship between the two. See Willmoore Kendall and George W. Carey, *The Basic Symbols of the American Political Tradition* (Baton Rouge, 1970), 155–56.

91. Clark, "The Supreme Court as a Protector of Liberty Under the Rule of Law," *Marquette Law Review* 43 (Summer 1959): 11, 15–16; Commager, *Freedom and Order: A Commentary on the American Political Scene* (New York, 1966), 11.

that will be needed if the United States is to achieve liberty and justice. "It is reasonable and moral," one argues, "for the American people to support both nonmaterialistic values and a system based upon property and liberty because these need not be incompatible with each other."[92]

Although the second sort of conclusion is closely related to the mutability and flux of the first, it retains a certain autonomy and may, perhaps, infuse these academic discussions with broader cultural implications. Americans have long been fascinated by, and enamoured of, "the blessings of liberty." Individuals as diverse as Charles Evans Hughes (in 1925), Charles A. Beard (in 1943), and Earl Warren (in 1955) have said so—all in so many words.[93] Early in 1982 ABC television presented "I Love Liberty," a musical-entertainment special that was described as a "celebration of American liberties." Although the program was organized by a liberal group led by Norman Lear, it was sufficiently nonpartisan to attract Barry Goldwater, Burt Lancaster, and Kenny Rogers as guests. More than 1,700 performers appeared in a lavish opening number that featured five marching bands, 16,000 red-white-and-blue balloons, and a 30-by-60-foot American flag.[94]

In 1944, when Learned Hand spoke in Central Park on the first "I Am an American Day," the substance of his brief address, called

92. Mark Silverstein, *Constitutional Faiths: Felix Frankfurter, Hugo Black, and the Process of Judicial Decision Making* (Ithaca, 1984), 182–83; Donald J. Devine, *Does Freedom Work? Liberty and Justice in America* (Ottawa, IL, 1978), viii; George H. Nash, *The Conservative Intellectual Movement in America since 1945* (New York, 1976), 64–65, 224, 236, 241. Cf. David Bollier, *Liberty and Justice for Some: Defending a Free Society from the Radical Right's Holy War on Democracy* (New York, 1982).

93. Hughes, "Liberty and Law," 183; Beard, *The Republic*, ch. 9; and Warren, "The Blessings of Liberty," *Washington University Law Quarterly*, vol. 1955 (April 1955), 105–11. The phrase "the blessings of liberty" appeared in the Virginia Bill of Rights in 1776.

94. *New York Times*, March 21, 1982, 27, 32. For a careful study that resulted in the conclusion that "ordinary" Americans have only vague and unsystematic notions concerning their freedoms, see Robert E. Lane, *Political Ideology: Why the American Common Man Believes What He Does* (New York, 1962), ch. 27, "Public Resources for Liberty and Justice." Lane found very little sense of injustice, and considerable confidence that the United States is a free country where those who deserve it enjoy justice.

"The Spirit of Liberty," was so eloquent and moving that the text became an object of wide demand. It was swiftly printed and reprinted in anthologies. Hand confessed in the talk that he really could not define the spirit of liberty. He knew that it did not mean complete freedom for the individual; yet he declared that liberty surely involved tolerance and the absence of dogmatic certainty that any individual enjoys a monopoly of ideological or moral rectitude. Ultimately, however, having denied that he *could* define liberty, Hand proceeded to do so by indirection, and in a manner not so far removed from Montesquieu. What is liberty? Hand's speculation became an affirmation by eloquent self-denial:

> It is not the ruthless, the unbridled will; it is not freedom to do as one likes. That is the denial of liberty, and leads straight to its overthrow. A society in which men recognize no check upon their freedom soon becomes a society where freedom is the possession of only a savage few.[95]

Hand may or may not have been aware that his guidelines remained very close to those of Montesquieu: "Liberty is not the power of doing as one likes, but rather the power of doing what one ought to wish to do; it is the right to do what the laws permit. It consists therefore of being governed by laws and of knowing that the laws will not arbitrarily be put on one side."[96]

A reductive label for the goals formulated by Montesquieu and Hand might very well be "liberty and justice." If those goals seem remarkably close to the framers' intent, we should not be surprised; for Montesquieu was one of the most influential sources of their thinking, and Learned Hand, assuredly, one of their most dedicated (as well as influential) disciples. It is no casual coincidence that the Preamble declares, early on, that the new government's major objectives included the establishment of justice and securing "the blessings of liberty to ourselves and our posterity."

The affirmation of liberty and justice is clearly not new; but it

---

95. Hand, "The Spirit of Liberty" (1944) in Dilliard, ed., *The Spirit of Liberty*, 189, 190.
96. Robert Shackleton, *Montesquieu: A Critical Biography* (Oxford, 1961), 287.

had to be rediscovered, in a sense, in response to the economic privation of the 1930s, the post–World War II recognition that all Americans did not enjoy liberty and justice, and the awareness that came in the 1950s that large numbers of Americans had become so apprehensive about the spectre of subversion that they were willing to subordinate liberty and justice to something less attractive than liberty and order: namely, the illusion of security.

We also needed to rediscover in the twentieth century what John Winthrop understood so well in the seventeenth, James Madison in the eighteenth, and Abraham Lincoln in the nineteenth: that liberty cannot be defined or appreciated as a singular quality. Walter Lippmann epitomized the point in 1920: "I can recall no doctrine of liberty," he wrote, "which, under the acid test, does not become contingent upon some other ideal."[97] That has, indeed, been the quintessential character of liberty's ever-changing role in American culture.

97. Lippmann, *Liberty and the News*, 21–22.

NOTES ON LIBERTY IN AMERICAN ICONOGRAPHY

INDEX

Notes on Liberty in American Iconography

These notes are intended to serve as a supplement to the text, and more particularly to the legends beneath the illustrations. Rather than attempt comprehensive coverage, the notes that follow simply provide leads to pertinent objects that are not shown, along with additional and contextual information about objects that are represented in the illustrations. Clearly, images of Liberty have permeated both high culture as well as folk and popular culture. In many instances it is impossible to draw a clear line of demarcation between them.

Historic Christ Church, founded in 1695 and located at Second Street above Market in Philadelphia, has a splendid stained-glass window known as the "Liberty Window." On the intricate upper panel, English barons accompanied by the Archbishop of Canterbury force a cowering King John to sign the Magna Carta on June 15, 1215. The lower panel shows the Rector of Christ Church opening the First Continental Congress with prayer in 1774.

For Liberty as a pervasive theme in the iconography of the American Revolution, see Donald H. Cresswell, comp., *The American Revolution in Drawings and Prints: A Checklist of 1765–1790 Graphics in the Library of Congress* (Washington, D.C., 1975). For an especially choice and representative example, see a mezzotint entitled "The Alternative of Williamsburg" (London, 1775), in which armed patriots compel recalcitrant merchants to sign agreements declaring that they will not import British goods. A child in the right foreground holds a pole with a banner bearing the word LIBERTY (reproduced in Rhys Isaac, *The Transformation of Virginia, 1740–1790* [Chapel Hill, 1982], figure XVI and p. 417).

Samuel Jennings's allegory of "Liberty Displaying the Arts and Sciences" (shown in figure 3) had several sources of inspiration in English libertarian thought. Thomas Gordon had written in "Cato's Letters," so familiar to the patriot cause, that "all good Arts and Sciences are produced by Liberty." See David L. Jacobson, ed., *The English Libertarian Heritage: From the Writings of John Trenchard and Thomas Gordon in "The Independent Whig" and "Cato's Letters"* (Indianapolis, 1965), 137–38.

A much larger version of Jennings's allegory (oil on canvas), also executed in London in 1792, is owned by the Library Company of Philadelphia. Most of the symbols associated with Miss Liberty are present: the liberty pole and cap, the broken chains at her feet, etc. See Robert C. Smith, "Liberty Displaying the Arts and Sciences: A Philadelphia Allegory by Samuel Jennings," *Winterthur Portfolio* 2 (1965): 84–105.

The Philadelphia Museum of Art owns two lead-glazed earthenware jugs, made in England for the American market, ca. 1800. One is decorated with a U.S. ship on one side and a bust of George Washington on the other, surrounded by the motto "Justice, Victory, and Liberty." The other jug is similar but also bears the words: "The Farmers Arms."

The popularity and influence of Edward Savage's 1796 painting and engraving, "Liberty in the form of the Goddess of Youth, giving support to the Bald Eagle," was extraordinary (see figures 5 and 7). For the original and an 1805 adaptation, see Joshua C. Taylor, *America as Art* (Washington, D.C., 1976), 12. For variations on the theme, some of them quite amusing, see Elinor Lander Horwitz, *The Bird, the Banner, and Uncle Sam: Images of America in Folk and Popular Art* (Philadelphia, 1976), 79–83; and Louis C. Jones, "Liberty and Considerable License," *Antiques* 74 (July 1958): 40–43. The Henry Ford Museum, Dearborn, Michigan, owns a version painted in gouache on glass by Abijah Canfield (ca. 1800–1810) in Chusetown (now Humphreysville), Connecticut.

The Abby Aldrich Rockefeller Folk Art Center in Williamsburg, Virginia, owns several versions based upon Savage's original. One was painted on velvet (ca. 1810). The Folk Art Center also has various other renditions of Liberty in the decorative arts: "Liberty Crowning Washington," a needlework and watercolor piece made on silk by Catharine Townsend Warner early in the nineteenth century; a watercolor of Miss Liberty (ca. 1815) on which is written "Liberty and Independence. Ever Glorious Memory"; and an intricate example of fine calligraphy based upon the eighteenth-century coat-of-arms of Pennsylvania. It bears the Pennsylvania state motto, "Virtue, Liberty and Independence," and is dated 1849.

For the pervasiveness and popularity of patriotic needlework (figures 4, 6–9), see Herbert R. Collins, *Threads of History: Americana Recorded on Cloth, 1775 to the Present* (Washington, D.C., 1979), esp. 96, 109, 193, 252, 301, 347, 349, 394.

The obsession with Miss Liberty, which reached its peak in American imagery between 1800 and 1815, was commented upon in various ways in contemporary correspondence. On March 10, 1806, for example, Fisher Ames wrote the following to Timothy Pickering of Massachusetts: "Our disease is democracy. It is not the skin that festers—our very bones are carious, and their marrow blackens with gangrene. Which rogues shall be first, is of no moment—our republicanism must die, and I am sorry for it. But why should we care what sexton happens to be in office at our funeral. Nevertheless, though I indulge no hopes, I derive much entertainment from the squabbles in Madam Liberty's family. After so many liberties have been taken with her, I presume she is no longer a *miss* and a virgin, though she may still be a goddess." Seth Ames, ed., *The Life and Works of Fisher Ames* (Boston, 1854), 1:369–70.

A great many Americans have carried Liberty in their purses and pockets because she appeared constantly on U.S. coinage throughout the century following Independence, and somewhat less commonly ever since. One of the best places to follow her changing visage is the National Numismatic Collection in the National Museum of American History, part of the Smithsonian Institution in Washington, D.C. Notable examples include the Liberty Cap cent designed by J. P. Droz (1793); the Liberty Head by Joseph Wright

(1793); the Liberty Head and Cap by Robert Scot (1794–96); the Draped Bust of Liberty by Scot after designs by Gilbert Stuart (1795–1808); the Liberty Bust by John Reich after designs by E. L. Persico (1807–34); the Liberty Head by Christian Gobrecht (1839–57); and the Seated Liberty by Gobrecht after designs by Thomas Sully (1837–41). Gobrecht worked as an engraver at the Philadelphia Mint from 1836 to 1844. His seated Liberty (see the frontispiece) has long been considered one of the most beautiful coin designs made during the nineteenth century.

By 1850 Liberty had appeared simultaneously on a considerable number of American coins, ranging from a copper penny to the famous $20 gold piece with a double eagle on the obverse side. The Liberty coinage in common use between 1849 and 1907 was designed by J. B. Longacre, who also engraved a Liberty Head with a feather head-dress (in use 1854–89). All of these coins are now highly valued by collectors, who are willing to pay extravagant prices for untarnished Liberty. In 1985, for example, a "gem brilliant" uncirculated 1825 "quarter eagle," or $2.50 gold piece, sold at auction for $55,000. One side bears the eagle rampant clutching three arrows in its talons. The obverse shows a bust of Miss Liberty surrounded by thirteen stars. She wears a rather scrunched liberty cap, at the base of which, just above her left ear, the word LIBERTY appears in bold letters. See *The New York Times*, April 14, 1985, sec. H, p. 38, "Numismatics."

Throughout the Civil War, "Union & Liberty" remained a popular slogan in the North. I have seen ordinary letter-writing paper from that period with an attractive design of Miss Liberty in the upper left-hand corner (more than 7 cm high on a sheet 20.5 cm long). She is demurely covered by elaborate drapery, wears an unscrunched liberty cap, holds an American flag topped by yet another liberty cap, and has the U.S. shield propped against her right leg.

During the later nineteenth century we get mixed signals from the sources concerning the relative prominence and popularity of Liberty in American material culture. One person, writing in the aftermath of the great Centennial Exhibition held at Philadelphia in 1876, explained that "the Stars and Stripes, the eagle, George Washington and the Goddess of Liberty compose a quartet which, no matter how artistically they may be combined, pall at the present time upon the general taste of the American public. . . ." See Jennie J. Young, "Ceramic Art of the Exhibition," in Edward C. Bruce, *The Century: Its Fruits and Its Festival* (Philadelphia, 1877), 247.

Completion of the Statue of Liberty in 1886 looks in retrospect like evidence to the contrary; but histories of the movement to erect such a statue, controversies over where to locate it, and how to raise money by public subscription for its pedestal and base, suggest that the Centennial in 1986 has generated considerably more enthusiasm (and money) than the original enterprise did during the 1870s and 1880s. See Marvin Trachtenberg, *The Statue of Liberty* (New York, 1976); Paul R. Baker, *Richard Morris Hunt* (Cambridge, MA, 1980), 314–22; and Bertha Pauli and E. B. Ashton, *I Lift My Lamp: The Way of a Symbol* (Port Washington, NY, 1948).

Despite current enthusiasm for refurbishing the Statue of Liberty, and the many tourists who have visited the exhibit pertaining to the history of American immigration displayed in the base of the Statue, there is little awareness of the Musée Bartholdi in Colmar, France, devoted to Fréderic Auguste Bartholdi and his lifelong dream: the Statue of Liberty as a gift from France to the United States. For an eclectic treatment of the origins of liberty in modern European iconography, see Jean Starobinski, *The Invention of Liberty, 1700–1789* (Geneva, 1964).

For just one example of the artifacts being produced commercially because of the Statue's Centennial, see *The New Yorker*, June 17, 1985, p. 72. The J. E. Caldwell Co. of Philadelphia and Washington is advertising an 18-inch figure of "Cybis" (Liberty). It sells for $1,875, "a portion of [the] proceeds to benefit [the] Liberty Park Monument Committee."

Among the papers of Cass Gilbert, chief architect of the U.S. Supreme Court Building in Washington, D.C., there are proposals from various sculptors who were commissioned to work on the marble friezes that surround the building. Robert Aitken of New York City, who carved the West Pediment, explained his design in these words:

> "Liberty" enthroned – looking confidently into the Future – across her lap the Scales of Justice – She is surrounded in the composition by two Guardian figures. On her right "Order" (the most active or alert of the two) scans the Future ready to detect any menace to Liberty. On her left "Authority" is shown in watchfull restraint yet ready to inforce, if necessary, the dictates of Justice. Then to the right and left of the Guardian figures groups of two figures each represent "Council." Then right and left two recumbent figures represent "Research" Past and Present.

> (Cass Gilbert Papers, box 15, Library of Congress, Manuscript Division, Washington, D.C.)

Illustrations 2, 5, 15, 16, 18, and 19 were located through (and made possible by) the Index of American Design, now based at the National Gallery of Art. For information about this ambitious project, which resulted in 17,000 watercolor renderings made between 1935 and 1942 of American decorative art objects, see Nancy E. Allyn, *The Index of American Design* (Washington, D.C., 1984), an informative and attractive booklet.

Index

Index

Harris, Robert J., 168
Hayek, Friedrich August von, 11*n*14
Henry, Patrick, 46
Hexter, J. H., 9
Hichborn, Benjamin, 36
Hobbes, Thomas, 15
Holmes, Oliver Wendell: on liberty of contract, 107; on vagueness of "liberty," 10, 103
Home, Henry, Lord Kames, 90
Hooker, Thomas, 20
Hoover, Herbert: *Challenge to Liberty, The,* 113
Hopkinson, Francis, 30
Howard, Martin, 34
Howe, Mark, 162
Hughes, Charles Evans: and "blessings of liberty," 170; on democracy and liberty, 147; on liberty of contract, 108, 109*n*93; and ordered liberty, 112, 115–16
Hume, David: *Federalist Papers* and, 41*n*57; on liberty and authority, 21; "Of the Origin of Government," 21
Hurst, J. Willard, 74
Hurtado v. California case (1884), 138–39
Hutchins, Robert M., 166
Hutchinson, Thomas, 11
Hyde, Edward, Viscount Cornbury, 26*n*20

Iconography of liberty, 175–80; illustrations of, 53–64, 117–26
"I love Liberty" (television program, 1982), 170
Independence and liberty, 67–68
"Independent Whig, The." *See* "Cato"
Indians (American), 22
Individualism: "Cato" on, 31
Individual liberty: Civil War and, 100; and freedom of contract, 106, 107; and government (Calhoun), 95; and privacy, 160; Roosevelt (F. D.) on, 129, 149; and social freedom, 84, 171; states

and, 143. *See also* Civil liberty; Personal liberty
Ireton, Henry, 24
Isolationism (American), 150

Jackson, Andrew, 162–63
Jackson, Robert H., 49, 157–58
Jay, John, 50–51, 127
Jefferson, Thomas: inaugural address (2nd, 1805), 79; on liberty and order, 79, 90; on liberty and property, 43; on separation of powers, 40
Jennings, Samuel, 26*n*20
Johnson, Andrew, 52 and *n*85
Johnson, Lyndon B., 157
Judges: on liberty and justice, 138–40, 152–54; on ordered liberty, 70–71. *See also* Supreme Court (U.S.)
Jurists. *See* Judges; Supreme Court (U.S.)
Justice, social: "Cato" on, 19; development of concept, 134; Hand (L.) on, 153–54; in Progressive Era, 140–41
Justice and liberty, 132–60; 18th century, 133–36; 19th century, 136–38; 20th century, 132–33, 139–60; antecedents of, 6; Cardozo on, 131 and *n*4; Coolidge on, 146; Frankfurter on, 153; relation to other sets, 5, 6, 132; Roosevelt (F. D.) on, 134, 149; Roosevelt (T.) on, 9, 140

Kames, Lord. *See* Home, Henry, Lord Kames
Kant, Immanuel, 49
Keller, Helen, 152
Kent, James: on liberty and justice, 137; on liberty and law and morality, 81; on liberty and property, 43
King, Rufus, 42

Labor: and Communist Party, 158; right of, to organize, 106, 109; right of, to strike, 101. *See also* Contract, liberty of
Landis, James M.: "Liberty as an Evolutionary Idea," 132–33

Index

Index

Index

Index

Wilson, James: on British sources of American notions of liberty, 4–5*n*4; on civil liberty, 22, 23; on "federal liberty," 51; "Of the Law of Nature," 37; on licentiousness and liberty, 73; on love of liberty, in America, 37

Wilson, Woodrow, 12; on liberty and authority, 71–72; on liberty and justice, 141; on liberty and order, 112

Winthrop, James, 46

Winthrop, John: "On Liberty," 20, 50

Wise, Henry A., 99

Wise, John, 20–21

Woman's liberty (18th century), 28

World War I, 141

"Yellow-dog" contracts, 105

Zenger, John Peter, 26

Also by Michael Kammen

A Season of Youth: The American Revolution and the Historical Imagination (1978)

Colonial New York: A History (1975)

People of Paradox: An Inquiry Concerning the Origins of American Civilization (1972)

Empire and Interest: The American Colonies and the Politics of Mercantilism (1970)

Deputyes & Libertyes: The Origins of Representative Government in Colonial America (1969)

A Rope of Sand: The Colonial Agents, British Politics, and the American Revolution (1968)

EDITOR

The Past Before Us: Contemporary Historical Writing in the United States (1980)

"What is the Good of History?" Selected Letters of Carl L. Becker, 1900–1945 (1973)

The History of the Province of New-York, by William Smith, Jr. (1972)

The Contrapuntal Civilization: Essays toward a New Understanding of the American Experience (1971)

Politics and Society in Colonial America: Democracy or Deference? (1967)

CO-AUTHOR

Society, Freedom, and Conscience: The American Revolution in Virginia, Massachusetts, and New York (1976)

CO-EDITOR

The Glorious Revolution in America: Documents on the Colonial Crisis of 1689 (1964)